CORPORATIONS OF CORRUPTION

CORPORATIONS OF CORRUPTION

A SYSTEMATIC STUDY OF

ORGANIZED CRIME

By

DAVID L. HERBERT, ESQ.

Partner, Herbert, Treadon, Benson & Frieg, Attorneys at Law, Canton, Ohio
Assistant Professor, Kent State University, Kent, Ohio
Former Assistant Chairman and Secretary, Ohio Governor's Law Enforcement
Consulting Committee on Organized Crime
Former Assistant County Prosecutor, Stark County (Canton) Ohio

and

HOWARD TRITT

Assistant Professor, Kent State University, Kent, Ohio
Coordinator, Criminal Justice Studies, Kent State University
Stark and Tuscarawas Campuses
Former Director, Criminal Justice Studies, Defiance College, Defiance, Ohio
Former Detective, Canton Police Department, Canton, Ohio

CHARLES C THOMAS • PUBLISHER
Springfield • Illinois • U.S.A.

Published and Distributed Throughout the World by

CHARLES C THOMAS • PUBLISHER
2600 South First Street
Springfield, Illinois 62717

With THOMAS BOOKS *careful attention is given to all details of manufacturing and design. It is the Publisher's desire to present books that are satisfactory as to their physical qualities and artistic possibilities and appropriate for their particular use.* THOMAS BOOKS *will be true to those laws of quality that assure a good name and good will.*

Printed in the United States of America

SC–R-3

Library of Congress Cataloging in Publication Data

Herbert, David L.
    Corporations of corruption.

    Bibliography: p.
    Includes index.
    1. Organized crime—United States.   2. Organized crime investigation—United States.   I. Tritt, Howard.
II. Title.
HV6791.H47   1984   364.1′06′073   83-24087
ISBN 0-398-04970-X

Although this work during the final completion stages was initially dedicated to my wife and children, my wife's mother suddenly and unexpectedly died just before the final type. My family's agony will not soon dissipate. My own fond remembrances of this fine and loving woman will certainly never be forgotten. With the sure and certain belief that her memory will never fade, I dedicate this work to a wonderful lady my children will always remember as "Granny": HONEY ANITA ROSENKRANZ.

David L. Herbert

The labors of man are many, the pleasures few. As one toils through life, one source provides him with the strength and substenance to continue. This source is man's most cherished possession. It is the love and support of his family. In humble response to this everlasting love and support, I dedicate this work to my wife Barbara and my children, Jodi, Michelle, and Scott.

Howard Tritt

INTRODUCTION

The study of organized crime involves more than the examination of simple criminal activity; it involves consideration of organized crime as a societal phenomena, as a business enterprise, and as a totalitarian, hierarchical government-like structure within government. It is not only an American phenomenon; it is an international problem. The threats posed by organized crime are many and varied. These threats affect the stability of our government as well as the vitality of our lives; they deeply affect our pocketbooks in many diverse and often complex ways and threaten our very health and safety. Yet, the vast majority of organized crime customers are willing purchasers of its unlawful goods and services. Moreover, due to recent organized crime efforts to infiltrate legitimate business, more and more of the world's citizens, including Americans in particular, undoubtedly will become unsuspecting organized crime customers as each year goes by. This is perhaps one of the biggest threats to arise from organized crime in the years to come.

Through insidious but very effective corruption of public officials, organized crime has gained a strong foothold in this country. In a letter to the Honorable James A. Rhodes, former Governor of the State of Ohio, Lt. David A. Dailey, Chairman of the 1982 Ohio Law Enforcement Consulting Committee on Organized Crime, concluded that organized crime groups have developed into "corporations of corruption," indeed in his opinion, "quasi-governments within our society, presenting a unique challenge to the administration of justice."[1] Lt. Dailey's astute comments have lead to the development of the title for this book. His accurate and

---

[1]Ohio Law Enforcement Consulting Committee, *Report to the Governor of Ohio on Organized Crime*, 1, (Columbus, Ohio, 1982).

keen observations are reflective of the overall and pervasive problem of organized crime.

Many governmental groups have examined the phenomena of organized crime, often in efforts to proscribe the activities carried on by organized crime. Year after year, decade after decade, their findings have been almost the same. In 1967, then President Lyndon Baines Johnson appointed a commission to study crime in America. This commission, the President's Commission on Law Enforcement and Administration of Justice, issued a report entitled "The Challenge of Crime in a Free Society." This report included an examination of organized crime, which in fact was the subject of a special Task Force Report from that Commission. The Commission, which engaged in perhaps the most exhaustive study of crime ever undertaken in this country, made the following conclusions:

> In many ways organized crime is the most sinister kind of crime in America. The men who control it have become rich and powerful by encouraging the needy to gamble, by luring the troubled to destroy themselves with drugs, by extorting the profits of honest and hardworking businessmen, by collecting usury from those in financial plight, by maiming or murdering those who oppose them, by bribing those who are sworn to destroy them. Organized crime is not merely a few preying upon a few. In a very real sense it is dedicated to subverting not only American institutions, but the very decency and integrity that are the most cherished attributes of a free society. As the leaders of Cosa Nostra and their racketeering allies pursue their conspiracy unmolested, in open and continuous defiance of the law, they preach a sermon that all too many Americans heed: The government is for sale; lawlessness is the road to wealth; honesty is a pitfall and morality is a trap for suckers.
>
> The extraordinary thing about organized crime is that America has tolerated it for so long.[2]

Similar conclusions were reached by other governmental groups preceding the President's Commission. In 1950, Senator Estes Kefauver, through a Senate Special Committee, began to investigate organized crime. By 1951, after hearings conducted all across the United States, this Committee had uncovered broad evidence of a massive, growing, interstate organized crime empire engaged in many illegal activities, as well as the bribery and corruption of

---

[2]The President's Commission on Law Enforcement and Administration of Justice. *The Challenge of Crime in a Free Society: A Report* (Washington D.C., 1967).

public officials. In 1957, a second congressional group, the Senate's Select Committee on Improper Activities in the Labor and Management Field, formed as a subcommittee of the Senate Committee on Government Operations, began to investigate organized crime in earnest. This Subcommittee, chaired by Senator John L. McClellan, found widespread evidence of organized crime involvement in labor unions and the misuse of labor union funds by such groups. Moreover, in the years following its initial formation, the "McClellan Subcommittee," as it commonly came to be known, produced a live witness, Joseph Valachi, who on national television testified as to the existence, structure, and innerworkings of a major organized crime group commonly called the "Mafia," or as he specifically referred to it "La Cosa Nostra," or "This Thing of Ours."

The revelations made by Mr. Valachi focused law enforcement efforts for the next twenty years mainly on La Cosa Nostra. Even the President's 1967 Crime Commission concentrated in many respects upon this group. By the mid 1970s, however, many authorities on organized crime began to consider and communicate the fact that Cosa Nostra was but one powerful organized crime group within the total realm of organized crime. As a partial result of such views, other organized crime groups began to come under increased scrutiny, study, and ultimate prosecution by law enforcement.

The traditional law enforcement response to the specter of organized crime has, for the most part, been reactive rather than prospective. However, commencing in the mid-1970s efforts were undertaken in earnest to direct law enforcement efforts to more prospective and aggressive investigations of organized crime, including its members and activities. As a consequence, many law enforcement departments have developed specialized intelligence units, which have begun to utilize modern investigative techniques and analysis methods to uncover evidence of organized crime's existence, activities, and memberships. Recent law enforcement efforts, for example, to infiltrate several organized crime groups upon the basis of information obtained through intelligence activities, have led to very successful prosecutions of various organized crime individuals, including high ranking members of La Cosa Nostra.

Change has come about somewhat slowly as to investigations and prosecutions of organized crime members. The 1980s and the 1990s may, in fact, prove to be the ultimate testing ground as to the continued existence or the ultimate extinction of many organized crime groups. Efforts are now underway at both the federal and state governmental levels to commit the necessary funds and investigative personnel to effectively deal with the problems of organized crime. The material provided in this book hopefully will assist the criminal justice, political science, or sociology student in understanding the overall workings of organized crime and the methods now in use or under development to deal with the problems of organized crime. A better trained, better equipped, and more knowledgeable law enforcement response to the problem of organized crime can only come about through increased understanding and knowledge. Hopefully, this work will contribute to that cause.

ACKNOWLEDGMENTS

Many people have made contributions in some manner to the production of this work. When I first became a lawyer, then Stark County Prosecuting Attorney and now United States District Judge for the Northern District of Ohio, David D. Dowd, Jr., former Ohio State Supreme Court Justice and former Chairman of the Ohio Organized Crime Prevention Council, hired me out of the University of Akron School of Law and brought me to Canton, Ohio, as one of his Assistant Prosecuting Attorneys. One of the first things he had me do was attend a seminar in 1975, in Columbus, Ohio, on the subject of organized crime. Although it was my first real exposure to the problems associated with organized crime, it piqued my interest in the subject and my search for understanding of the problem began in earnest. The following year, I was elected Secretary of the Ohio Organized Crime Prevention Council's Law Enforcement Consulting Committee from law enforcement officers throughout the State of Ohio. Eventually I served as Assistant Chairman of that group. The Honorable David D. Dowd, Jr., is therefore responsible for my interest in this subject and consequently responsible for this work in a very direct way. His long standing guidance and original direction in this area, as well as many others, has made a very significant impact upon my life; that guidance and direction must be and is hereby warmly acknowledged.

The former Ohio Organized Crime Council staff assistants over the years must also be acknowledged, as they contributed in many ways to the development of this book, especially the friendship and assistance of Dr. Edmund G. James, Jr., former Director of the council staff.

The assistance of William Downerd, Secret Service Officer for the Stark County Prosecuting Attorney's Office, is also acknowledged. Special mention should be made of the fact that Bill has devoted a good part of his life to the investigation and prosecution of organized crime figures. His conduct has always been exemplary and should be followed by more in his field.

Research assistance for this work was provided by my law clerks, and Steve Struhar and Margaret Gardner, both law students at the University of Akron, School of Law, and two very able and capable college students, Linda Shalosky, now a law student at the University of Akron, School of Law, and Paula Hackathorn, a Criminal Justice Studies student at Kent State University. Typing was provided by Lori Bellay, Brenda Holland, and Carolyn Greer. Copying and assorted assistance at all stages was provided by Brenda Holland. All of these individual's assistance over many months is gratefully acknowledged and appreciated.

David L. Herbert

CONTENTS

CORPORATIONS OF CORRUPTION

Section I
History and Organization
of Organized Crime

Chapter 1

ORGANIZED CRIME DEFINED

In order to properly and accurately study the phenomenon of organized crime, it is first necessary to define it, examine its basic characteristics, and in the process "weed out" any lingering misconceptions about it. This is no easy task. Sociologists, anthropologists, legislators, judges, law enforcement personnel, and other commentators have all had great difficulty in defining organized crime. Numerous conferences as well as Congressional Committees have made attempts to promulgate proposed definitions. Many of these definitions have fallen short of their goal or have become overladen with ethnic overtones, thereby continuing stereotypical myths that have little application to today's organized crime problems; others have either failed to reach a workable, uniformly accepted definition or have been drafted so broadly and so vaguely as to fail to pass constitutional muster. All of these failings have greatly hampered accurate study and analysis of the problem.

For many years it was impossible to convince certain law enforcement personnel that organized crime even existed and no less to develop a workable, universally accepted definition for it. Such views are not totally dispersed even today. However, significant attempts have been made to define the problem; such attempts must serve as starting points for any study of the problem as well as the development of any meaningful measures designed to eliminate that problem.

Commonly, organized crime is often defined as a "cancer," "malignancy," "disease," or "plague." Mob insiders, as well as economists, often define organized crime as a "business," "enterprise," "organization," or even "corporation" or "company." Law enforcement officers often talk of "making war against it," while other law abiding citizens prepare themselves to be entertained by it. Many fear it, while many are harmed, scared, and killed by it. It has untold wealth, power, and influence. It is corrupt and at the same time corrupting. It is clearly organized and certainly secretive. It is criminal as well as perverse. It, as we shall see, exists despite the problems associated with defining it, which often hinge upon analogies like the foregoing for the definitions own "success" in the face of practical definitional perplexities.

Although efforts were made as early as 1931 by the presidentially appointed Wickersham Commission to define organized crime, serious efforts to define the enterprise were not undertaken until the 1950s and the 1960s when Congressional Committees began to uncover evidence of a secret criminal society or cartel called "the Mafia" or "La Cosa Nostra." In 1950, a Senate Special Committee to Investigate Organized Crime in Interstate Commerce was formed, and Senator Estes Kefauver was appointed Chairman. This Committee, however, focused on the "Mafia" for its definitional underpinnings and concentrated on a study of monolithic, centralized control of all organized crime activities in America. The definitional offerings put forth by the Committee were thus open to criticism and ultimate failure inasmuch as the definitional attempts were too narrow and restrictive in part, while at the same time the total organizational control for organized crime was overestimated and overstated.

Despite the Kefauver Committee's definitional shortcomings, another Senate Investigation's revelations in the 1960s lent credence to the Kefauver Committee findings. The Senate Subcommittee on Investigations of the Senate Government Operations Committee, chaired by Senator John L. McClellan, brought forth testimonial proof in 1963 of the existence of "La Cosa Nostra" (our thing). Joseph Valachi, a Subcommittee witness and a "made member" himself, testified at great length about the organizational structure, personnel, business, strengths, and weaknesses of his organization. His detailed and sometimes chilling descriptions of La Cosa Nostra contributed to the adherence to a somewhat narrow, ethnic oriented, and centralized definitional description for organized crime. Supporters of such definitions could thus cite both the Kefauver and the McClellan Committee findings in support of their positions. Moreover, the chance discovery in 1957 of a national meeting of ethnic criminal cartel (Cosa Nostra) chieftains in the Appalachian Mountains in New York state further lent support to such definitional theories.

In 1965, two rather significant actions began that lead to a more workable and accurate definition for organized crime. First, on July 23, 1965, President Lyndon B. Johnson issued Executive Order No. 11236, which established a national Commission on Law Enforcement and Administration of Justice. Two years later the Commission reported to the President in its publication, *The Challenge of Crime In A Free Society, A Report By the President's Commission on Law Enforcement and Administration of Justice* (February 1967) (hereinafter referred to as *Report.*) That *Report* also included a more concentrated publication, *The Task Force Report on Organized Crime* (1967), (hereinafter referred to as *Task Force Report*). The *Report*, although emphasizing the roll of the "Mafia" or "La Cosa Nostra," expanded prior definitional references and clearly provided a somewhat more workable definition for organized crime:

> Organized crime is a society that seeks to operate outside the control of the American people and their governments. It involves thousands of criminals, working within structures as complex as those of any large corporation, subject to laws more rigidly enforced than those of legitimate governments. Its actions are not impulsive but rather the result of intricate conspiracies, carried on over many years and aimed at gaining control over whole fields of activity in order to amass huge profits.
>
> The core of organized crime activity is the supplying of illegal goods and services—gambling, loansharking, narcotics and other forms of vice—to countless numbers of citizen customers. But organized crime is also extensively and deeply involved in legitimate business and in labor unions. Here it employs illegitimate methods—monopolization, terrorism, extortion, tax evasion—to drive out or control lawful ownership and leadership and to exact illegal profits from the public. And to carry on its many activities secure from governmental interference, organized crime corrupts public officials.[1]

Second, in 1965, then New York Governor Nelson A. Rockefeller

---

[1]The President's Commission on Law Enforcement and Administration of Justice, *The Challenge of Crime in a Free Society: A Report*, 187 (Washington D.C., 1967).

began to bring together knowledgeable and experienced people to confer upon the problems associated with organized crime. These gatherings continued until 1967 and are commonly known as the Oyster Bay Conferences on Combating Organized Crime. The Conferees initial problems centered upon achieving a definition for organized crime that would ultimately contribute to effective law enforcement responses to the problem. The group shifted significantly away from descriptions of prior organized crime personalities or ethnic groups or traits and began to concentrate on organized crime as a phenomenon and not just a single ethnic entity.

The Oyster Bay Conferences produced several different bases for a logical progression and evolution of prior definitions. Generally, the conferees defined organized crime by identifying its salient characteristics:

1. Self-perpetuating, totalitarian, continuing criminal conspiracies.
2. Designed for profit and power by preying upon human weaknesses.
3. Utilizing fear and corruption.
4. Seeking to obtain immunity from the laws.

The Conference ultimately concluded that organized crime was a business venture, operating much like a corporation but with a limited and highly profitable membership and possessing quite effective persuasive tools: fear, threat, intimidation, murder, and corruption. The conferees also concentrated upon the inner workings of such groups and found strict codes of behavior, diversification of responsibilities, hierarchical and totalitarian structures, several levels of management and responsibility, internal controls and enforcement, and several insulating levels within the structure, much like a government within a government.

The Oyster Bay Conference findings were a significant step toward a more comprehensive and workable definition for organized crime. As a practical matter, the Conference honed in on certain characteristics that are extremely useful not only to the development of an enforcement response to the criminal activity but also for the study of the problem.

In 1976, The National Advisory Committee on Criminal Justice Standards and Goals issued its *Report of the Task Force on Organized Crime.* That report offered definitional descriptions for organized crime focusing upon it's criminal and internal characteristics and concluded that organized crime was not synonymous with the Mafia or LaCosa Nostra.[2]

Some State Commissions have also made attempts to arrive at generally accepted definitional references for organized crime. In 1980, Pennsylvania issued its 1980 *Organized Crime Report.* That report offered the following definition for organized crime:

> Organized crime: The unlawful activity of an association trafficking in illegal goods or services, including but not limited to gambling, prostitution, loansharking, controlled substances, labor racketeering or other unlawful activities or any continuing criminal conspiracy or other unlawful practice which has as its objective large economic gain through fraudulent or coercive practices or improper governmental influence.[3]

In 1982, The Ohio Law Enforcement Consulting Committee in its *Report to the Governor of Ohio* formulated this definition:

> Organized crime, in the traditional sense, can be defined as a group of persons who operate outside the law for a purpose of financial gain, in a continuing criminal conspiracy, and who have the ability for political corruption and control to further their cause. They operate illegal enterprises and also invest their monies in legitimate businesses. The group manifests itself primarily in the areas of narcotics, gambling, loansharking, labor racketeering, extortion, major burglaries and robberies. This authoritarian group maintains a rigid control within the organization, an organization sometimes so well disciplined that it does not hesitate to employ disciplinary action such as beatings, bombings, or killings in order to maintain control of its resources to corrupt government officials and, therefore, control the governmental processes, using it to their own advantages, in the furtherance of their power.[4]

Similar definitions have been promulgated in many other states,

---

[2]National Advisory Committee on Criminal Justice Standards and Goals, *Report of the Task Force on Organized Crime* (1976).

[3]Pennsylvania Crime Commission, *A Decade of Organized Crime: 1980 Report*, 3 (1980).

[4]Ohio Law Enforcement Consulting Committee, *Report to the Governor of Ohio on Organized Crime* (1982).

missions or quasi-public groups. Some committees have defined including California, New Jersey, and New York by various comorganized crime by reference to "white collar crime." Such analogies are really misplaced. Organized crime, unlike white collar crime, is the principal business or occupation of its participants, while white collar crime is incidental crime associated with another business or occupation, in which crime is committed during the course of such business or occupation.

For our purposes and borrowing upon all prior definitional attempts, organized crime can consequently be aptly defined and analyzed by an examination of its six basic characteristics:

1. A conspiratorial entity, composed of two or more persons, acting as a group;
2. Formed and existing with the purpose to engage in illegal activities or the infiltration of legitimate business through illegal means;
3. Formed and existing for the acquisition of profit or power to assist in the acquisition of profit;
4. Through the corruption of governmental officials;
5. With the least possible risk; and
6. On an ongoing, self-perpetuating basis.

By utilization of such a definitional model, organized crime can be studied by not only examining its criminal activities but also by examining its socioeconomic workings and impact. Moreover, the breadth of the study becomes more accurate, more realistic, and clearly more useful. Old theories, definitionally limiting examination to particular ethnic groups, are simply and clearly misplaced. Organized crime is really a much larger sphere than the Mafia or La Cosa Nostra, which are but subspheres themselves within the larger sphere of organized crime. Moreover, the definitional framework used herein does not restrict the study to geographical areas, particular activities, or similar limiting factors.

This definitional scheme however, is not all inclusive. For example, "normal" criminal activity is clearly excluded. Crimes of passion or impulse, street muggings, rape, and similar activities, even though committed perhaps by a group, are normally outside our definitional reference. Such groups do not fit into the definitional model unless of course all six characteristics are present. Moreover, group criminal activity committed for political or terrorist purposes also is excluded from our definitional reference inasmuch as such groups are not motivated economically but rather are motivated politically.

To demonstrate the model and the interrelationship of a few of the identified organized crime groups as well as the interrelationships of such groups to certain other segments of society, Figure 1 might be useful. Proper pictorial display of the usefulness of a more accurate definition of organized crime should assist in the overall comprehension of the scope of this study.

It should become apparent from this diagram that organized

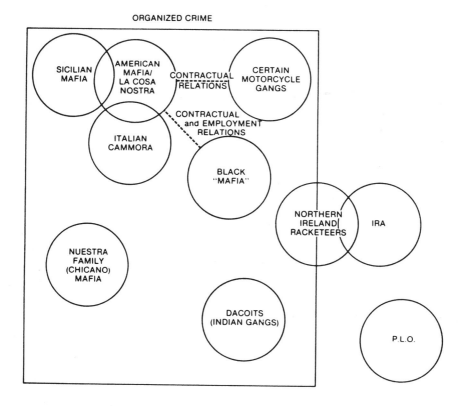

Figure 1. Interrelationships of selected organized crime groups.

crime has within its sphere many subgroups, of which the American Mafia or La Cosa Nostra is but one. It should also be noted, for example, that some groups might be related to one another, but not necessarily the same, e.g., Sicilian Mafia—American Mafia/La Cosa Nostra. Additionally, it is important to realize that there are some groups not clearly or totally within the definitional reference because of confusion regarding one or more of their characteristics, e.g., Northern Ireland Racketeers reportedly operate primarily to benefit the IRA and to bankroll the IRA's guerilla activities and not just for profits or economic power; thus their clear inclusion within the sphere of organized crime groups is not possible.

Interrelationships can exist between various organized crime groups or between an organized crime group and a nonorganized crime group. For example, the Mafia/La Cosa Nostra often employs motorcycle gang members or other specialized segments of organized crime for certain contract killings, even though the executioners are not "made" members of the employer's group ("made" members of the Mafia/Cosa Nostra are those who are formally inducted into the group).

As we shall see in Chapter 3, clear distinctions within each group serve to segregate and in some respects separate each such group, but in doing so, the six characteristic definitional model does not change. In other words, differences in internal management, codes of behavior, dress code, ethnic backgrounds, and enforcement rules or such similar sociological or organizational processes do not alter the inclusion of all properly identified groups within the total sphere of organized crime.

Even though the advancement of a definitional model as a reference point for the study of organized crime can be adapted readily for our own purposes, a similar advancement of the reference to prohibit such activity *criminally* is much more difficult. Although we are able to promulgate such a definition for examinational purposes, legislation proscribing certain criminal activity, punishable by fine and/or imprisonment, must pass certain constitutional requirements, including equal protection, specificity, clearness, and due process. As we shall see in Chapters 7 and 8, this is no easy task. Senator McClellan recognized the problems involved in such legislative drafting when he began to consider a legislative response to his Committee's findings about the Mafia and organized crime. His efforts at drafting a law to criminalize, in essence, active membership in such organizations were very strenuously chastised by, among others, the then Attorney General of the United States, largely because of the constitutional problems associated with the proposed law.

Legislative efforts to criminally proscribe organized criminal conduct have progressed since Senator McClellan's attempts. In fact such efforts have come to fruition in some cases, without violation of constitutional safeguards. Thus, workable, realistic, viable, and useful, but constitutional, definitions for organized criminal activity have been developed, which, although similar to our six characteristic model, are sufficiently specific and clear as to allow their use for criminal prosecution.

Chapter 2

HISTORY OF ORGANIZED CRIME

INTRODUCTION

A s we have seen, there are many varied and diverse definitions of "organized crime" depending upon the elemental character- istics utilized in establishing the definition itself. When examin- ing the historical origins and the evolution of organized crime many perspectives can be utilized: religious, political, sociological, economic, legal, ethnic, and others. It is often difficult to deter- mine which groups or events should be evaluated when studying the historical backdrop of organized crime, especially in light of modern definitional concepts. Nevertheless, a workable frame- work for historical examination can be developed to allow exami- nation of groups and events of the past, important to an overall understanding of organized crime. However, concrete evolution or clear development of organized crime from "old" to "new" is difficult, if not impossible.

Many scholars have attempted to develop concrete correlations associating a particular contemporary organized crime group to a particular group or groups of the past; such associations appear to be based largely upon subjective supposition rather than facts. Unlike such subjective approaches, the historical discus- sion presented herein should illustrate the differing interpreta- tions and diverse evolutionary considerations to be taken into account in examining the historical backdrop of contemporary organized crime groups. Therefore, the following materials should be studied objectively so that the reader avoids the pitfalls of interpreting any data as absolute.

Although there are numerous points throughout history that could be used as a starting point for any discussion as to the origins of organized crime, it seems best to begin with an examination of certain components of four basic civilizations: the Moslems, the Chinese, the Mongols, and the Christians.

The Moslems

Following the death of Mohammed in 632 AD, the struggle for power in the Moslem world began in earnest. One group vying for power was the Ismailians, also known as the Molahids or the "Lost Ones." Through their apostles, members of this group were indoctrinated in certain secret orders and wisdoms based upon Greek, Palestinian, and Persian philosophies at the "House of Science," which was located in an area where Cairo, Egypt, is now located. Gradually, their beliefs spread throughout the Moslem world.[1]

One prominent apostle, Hassan Ben Sabak, founded his own sect of Eastern Ismailians based upon a philosophy of atheism, immorality, vengeance, and strict obedience under punishment of death for violation of secret doctrines. The followers' fanatical dedication to Sabak's ideologies and their innate brutality, including terrorism and killing, soon caused the sect to become a powerful political, social, and religious force. The Eastern Ismailians developed what could be called the "art of killing." The name for such acts was "assassination," and the weapon used was the dagger. The actual assassination tactics then developed are still of some import as many of these are still employed without much basic change, save on occasion, for the weapon to be utilized.

This assassination scenario developed basically as follows: The subject's routine was studied to find the most appropriate time and place for the attack; the time was often dictated by the place selected, and in many cases a public place was chosen for the assassination so that the target would feel most secure and least suspecting of an attack. Once the time and place were selected, a team of assassins, usually six individuals, were selected to attack in two waves. The objective of the first wave was to kill, if possible, and if not, to cause a state of confusion. The second wave of three would watch, and if the first wave was not successful in inflicting fatal injuries the second wave would strike swiftly using the confused state created by the first wave to shield their actions.

---

[1]J. Curtin, *The Mongols: A History*, pp. 197–208 (Boston, Little Brown & Co., 1908).

Sabak's sect became known as "the assassins." Their reign of corruption, terror, and assassination continued for many years throughout the Moslem world until the Mongolian leader Hulagu broke their criminal domination and scattered them into small bands whose descendents, some feel, still exist today. Clearly, however, their ultimate enforcement rules, tactics, penalties, and secret codes of criminal conduct continue through this day and have been passed on to more contemporary organized crime groups.

The Chinese

In Chinese history, two secret societies predominate any historical organized crime examination: The White Lotus Society and the Hung Society. The White Lotus Society is believed to have been founded in Northern China as a peasant religious order. This group spawned many splinter sects including The Red Scarf Society, The Eight Trigram Society, The Yellow Society, The Boxers, The Society of the White Robe and The Tsai-li.[2] Although originally religious societies, many of these splinter sects underwent a metamorphosis in the face of adverse governmental oppression and began the use of criminal tactics for retribution.[3]

The Hung Society had its beginnings in the political arena and was believed founded in 1631 by Yin Hung-sheng in south, west, and central China. It, too, had many separate groups or sects; however, two were most prominent: The Triple Harmony Society, also known as the Triad Society (which many years later merged with the Chik Kung Tong Society in the United States) and the Elder Society.[4]

Although again founded for seemingly legitimate purposes, members of the Triad participated in rebellious activities against the British government and certain Christian missionaries in efforts to save the Chinese Imperial throne; however, gambling,

---

[2]W. DeBary, et al., ed., *Sources of Chinese Tradition*, pp. 639–641 (New York, Columbia University Press, 1960).

[3]J. Macgowan, *The Imperial History of China*, pp. 553 (New York, Barnes & Noble Books, 1973).

[4]W. DeBary, *supra* note 2 at 651.

opium trade, prostitution, and other illegal activities of the society continued under the auspices of such virtuous activities.[5]

The other Hung Society subsect, The Elder Society, was believed to have originated in Central China around 1850. They were also political, formed to resist the Manchus of South China. They became so powerful, well organized, and influential that many leading governmental officials were obligated to become members of the society.[6] It is reported that remnants of these societies are still active not only in China but in the United States as well. However, the use of covers or even governmental officials for the furtherance of the illegal activities are indeed still prevalent in modern organized crime groups.

The Mongols

The Mongols were a warring nomadic tribal people who survived on the fruits of battle acquired in their attacks on neighboring peoples. The Mongols influenced the entire civilized world during their period of power. However, their reign over very large geographic areas was often loose, allowing local, unscrupulous individuals to organize and exploit their own people. Although many of these groups were legitimate, some were not. These groups capitalized on the fears and ignorance of their followers to turn their frustrations on local governments in an endeavor to neutralize the government's power and quench their own thirst for power and wealth. The Mongols reign of terror spread over almost 1,000 years and deeply entrenched certain criminal groups and methods. Those groups' utilization of weak government to foster their own criminal goals, however, outlasted even a thousand year reign.

The Christians

Following a sermon by Pope Urban II in 1095, the Christian effort to free the Holy Lands from infidel oppression began. This effort, commonly known as the Crusades, included the entire spectrum of European society.[7] As each crusade lost its initial

---

[5]A. Daraul, *A History of Secret Societies*, p. 244 (New York, Citadel Press, 1961).

[6]W. DeBary, *supra* note 2 at 651.

[7]H. Lamb, *The Crusades*, p. 63 (Garden City, New Jersey, Doubleday & Company, 1930).

impetus, as well as many of its initial goals, many of the less fortunate crusaders, unable to finance their return to Europe, turned to criminal activities to survive. Others headed for the hills and mountains of either Cyprus or Sicily. In both cases, displaced crusaders soon learned that local governments were unable or unwilling to protect or care for them. By banding into various organized groups, they managed to survive and protect themselves, primarily through secret criminal societies.

WORLD HISTORY

Aside from the societal segments already analyzed, examples of people and events affecting the historical development of organized crime and its methods permeate the history of all societies. In England and France, criminal elements of the Elizabethan period formed themselves into government-like structures with their own codes. Similar organizations operated through all areas of Europe, Asia Minor, and the Mediterranean. One of the most heinous of those bands was the Decided Ones of Jupiter. Formed around 1815 near Calabria and Abruzzi, this band of outlaws and murderers terrorized the countryside for many years. Their leader, Ciro Annunchiarico, is alleged to have killed between sixty to seventy individuals before his capture and subsequent execution. At the group's peak in 1818, it is estimated that they had 20,000 members.

Like Europe, Southeast Asia and India had their own organized gangs, including the Phansegars that robbed and murdered travelers for their livelihood. Many of these criminals used menial jobs to serve as covers for their illegal activities.[8]

India was the chief supplier of opium for the rest of the world during the eighteenth and nineteenth centuries. Organized crime groups as well as governmental leaders were quick to capitalize upon this rich source of cash revenue. For example, in 1772, the British Governor of Bengal, Warren Hastings, sold concessions for the production, harvest, and sale of the product to raise revenues for the colonial operation. Much of this opium export went

---

[8]F. Homer, *Guns and Garlic*, p. 30 (West Lafayette, Ind., Purdue University Press, 1974).

to China, which had outlawed opium smoking in 1729.[9]

The one organized crime group that has received the most notoriety is the so-called Mafia. The term "Mafia," as used especially in America, may not in fact even be the correct term for the organization to which it refers. Evidence has been put forth indicating that the Mafia is known among its members as "La Cosa Nostra" rather than Mafia. La Cosa Nostra simply means "this thing of ours." The term Mafia, moreover, may have become an almost generic term for description of various organized crime groups including those now labeled as the "Israeli Mafia" the "Black Mafia," the "Chicano Mafia," etc.

Although there is some disagreement among the authorities, there is some evidence that suggests that secret criminal societies in Sicily did exist from time to time but often with different motives and goals. Some authorities trace the historical development of today's Mafia to revenge societies formed in Sicily, perhaps as early as 1200 AD, in response to continuing governmental takeovers of the island and use of the island as a stepping stone to Italy and efforts to conquer Europe. Others contend that only one organization, known as the Mafie, ever existed in Sicily and that this organization with its secret code of behavior was transported to America during the 1800s immigration from Sicily and Italy.

In Italy, however, it is quite clear that a secret criminal society was formed in Naples called the Camorra. The Camorra also developed a secret code of behavior that was definitely transported to the United States during the 1800s immigration. The Camorra continues to exist and thrive in Italy today.

Membership in either organization was based upon a strict code of behavior, which included the following:

1. To render all possible aid to a fellow member;
2. To swear absolute obedience to the superior;
3. To avenge an offense against any member as an offense against all;
4. To keep secret the names and procedures of the society; and

---

[9]A. McCoy, et al., *The Politics of Heroin in Southeast Asia*, p. 366–368 (New York, Harper & Row, 1972).

5. To refrain from ever appealing to state authorities for redress.[10]

Various attempts by governmental entities, including in Italy and Sicily, to abolish the Mafia were largely unsuccessful. However, during the 1920s, Cesare Mori, Benito Mussolini's Chief of Police, started a campaign to rid Italy of secret criminal groups, and by 1928 he boasted that this feat had been accomplished. Nevertheless, by 1943, during World War II, as the Allies prepared to invade Sicily, the combined aid and control of "Lucky" Luciano, an American Mafioso, and Calogero Vizzini, also known as "Don Calo," then head of the Sicilian Mafia, provided the allies with one of their cheapest and most decisive victories.[11] In return for Don Calo's assistance, the Allied forces made Don Calo Mayor of Villalba and put into positions of power those Mafioso he recommended as anti-fascists and true Italian patriots. Thus they delivered Sicily back into the hands of the Mafia, from which Mussolini had almost delivered it."[12]

AMERICAN HISTORY

Organized crime in America, although not a direct transplant from the Old World, has existed since colonial times. Prior to the 1920s, American organized crime groups were dominated by great and powerful Irish and Jewish gangs. During Prohibition, which went into effect with the passage of the Eighteenth Amendment to the United States Constitution and the subsequent enactment of the Volstead Act in 1920, Italian and Sicilian gangs began to rise to positions of prominence and began to compete with the powerful Irish, Jewish, and other major organized crime gangs of the times.

Prior to 1920, distinct ethnic gangs operated in America individually and in competition with one another. The Sicilian immigrants operated under the auspices of Mafia gangs, while the Italian immigrants operated under the auspices of Camorra gangs. However, organized crime activities during Prohibition, as well as

---

[10]W. Whalen, Handbook of Secret Organizations, p. 101 (New York, MacMillan Publishing Co., Inc., 1966).

[11]N. MacKenzie, ed., Secret Societies, pp. 253–255 (New York, Holt, Rinehart & Winston, 1967).

[12]*Id* at 255.

a series of Mafia-Camorra gang wars, convinced organized crime leaders that cooperation rather than competition would ultimately benefit all. Consequently, by 1930, any remaining distinction between the Mafia, primarily composed of ethnic Sicilian gangsters, and the Camorra, primarily composed of ethnic Italian gangsters, was largely dissipated and a unified Mafia now commonly known as La Cosa Nostra emerged as perhaps the most powerful American organized crime group of all time. The basic Cosa Nostra code of behavior as well as its enforcement tools and methods of operation developed by a wide variety of earlier organized crime groups were readily utilized by this unified group, as well as its predecessor organizations.

Aside from these early immigrant crime groups, other immigrants brought with them different criminal societies and codes of behavior, many of which continue to operate in some sections of the United States and on an international basis. Among these is the Chinese Tong, which still operates in many American cities. The Tong began its early rackets in the United States around 1905 primarily in New York City. Conflicts between various Chinese Tong groups emerged in a series of bloody wars among the various factions. Eventually, the results of the conflicts between the various Tong groups resulted in peaceful co-existence and mutual cooperation.

With the passage of the Eighteenth Amendment to the United States Constitution (thereby creating Prohibition) and the Volstead Act (thereby making the manufacture, transportation, sale, or consumption of alcoholic beverages criminal), organized crime was given a major and lucrative incentive to begin in earnest certain criminal activities, including the importation and distribution of illegal liquor from Canada and Mexico as well as Europe. Consequently, by the end of Prohibition in 1933, with the Twenty-first Amendment to the United States Constitution, organized crime had grown into a powerful and financially stable empire. With the end of Prohibition, for example, the emerged and united Mafia-Camorra group was composed of twenty-four core groups, with approximately 5,000 hard-core "made" (formally inducted) members. The consolidation of the Mafia into the twenty-four crime families was achieved through the efforts of "Lucky" Luciano, a rather infamous American gangster, who on September 10, 1931, reportedly arranged to have forty Mafia crime leaders across the entire United States assassinated almost simultaneously. That night, which has come to be known as the "Night of the Sicilian Vespers," solidified the organizational structure of organized crime that has continued to this day.

Along with the rise and organization of the Mafia crime groups during Prohibition, the previously powerful Irish and Jewish gangs' influence and stature gradually diminished. Members of these groups were rapidly assimilated into American society. Consequently, the assimilation of such individuals into the mainstream of American society, coupled with the rise to power of the Mafia crime groups, led to the Irish and Jewish gangs' ultimate demise.

Prohibition also vaulted various Mafia organized crime groups into positions of power and influence through corruption and bribery of public officials. The corruption, despite the loss of vast cash profits acquired during Prohibition, continued after 1933 and the repeal of Prohibition. During the time period commencing with 1933, organized crime began to concentrate on the return of profits through its gambling and prostitution activities, which also concomitantly developed along with the illegal liquor trade during Prohibition. Gambling, alcohol, and prostitution seemed to play off of and benefit one another and were often provided in conjunction with one or the other of these three basic activities. Investments, for example, in alcohol importation systems also frequently led to the further investment of organized crime group funds. Gambling casinos in Cuba first used as a staging area for alcohol importation into the United States were thus acquired during Prohibition. However, these were lost once Fidel Castro overthrew the Cuban government in 1959, previously headed by Fulgencio Batista, who theretofore encouraged mob investment in Cuban casinos. Slowly but surely, from 1933 through the 1960s, organized crime began (despite earlier efforts to curb such activities) to engage in drug trafficking operations. Ultimately, such activities would prove to be organized crime's most lucrative business venture. The smuggling methods learned during Prohibition would prove to be valuable tools for organized crime groups, readily adaptable to illicit drug trafficking. Moreover, the transportation, trucking, and distribution system developed by organized crime for the importation of illegal alcohol during Prohibition would provide an easy method for infiltration of organized crime groups into legitimate business activities. In addition, the conversion of an illegal enterprise to a legitimate one would lend convenient covers to organized crime's ongoing criminal operations and, at the same time, provide respectable employment for many of the group's members.

Between 1900 and the end of Prohibition in 1933, early American labor organizational efforts were faced with rather stiff and often violent employer opposition. Some of these embryonic labor unions often turned to organized crime for assistance in opposing employer-led violence. Organized crime, consequently, lent its muscle, experience, and reputation for violence to these emerging and struggling labor unions. A bond between the two groups thus developed that has endured in many unions to this day. Although early cooperative efforts between the two may have assisted to some degree in labor's early organizational efforts, that initial cooperation has changed so that the original servant has now become the current master. Organized crime began in earnest to dip into the rather substantial union treasuries following Prohibition. A variety of devices were used to siphon off millions of dollars from a variety of labor union pension, welfare and other member benefit funds. Some of the affected unions, including many say the powerful Teamsters Union, may have become dominated in some respects by organized crime elements. The historical bond formed many years ago has been manipulated by organized crime to its great present-day benefit.

CONCLUSION

The wealth and power of modern American organized crime groups, gained during and as a result of Prohibition, catapulted organized crime into the rest of the twentieth century as a viable, self-sustaining criminal force. The methods of operation borrowed from early crime groups and entrenched during Prohibition continue to serve organized crime to this day. The groups' continuing fulfillment of public desires for illegal goods and services while insulated from prosecution by a vast network of crooked governmental servants protects these corporations of corruption. So it has been; so it may continue to be.

Chapter 3

STRUCTURE AND PHILOSOPHY
OF ORGANIZED CRIME

M ost individual organized crime groups are centralized, hierarchical, authoritarian, and secret organizations. The groups
typically have centralized management, several insulating levels
of responsibility and decision making, and concentration of power
at the top level positions. Moreover, the groups are often characterized by divisions of labor and responsibility.

Organized crime groups are distinct from other crime groups
because of their formal, organized, and self-perpetuating structures.
Much like legitimate business entities, such groups must conform
to certain basic tenets of organization; however, organized crime is
distinguished from legitimate business groups because of its methods
of operation as well as its problem-solving "alternatives." By developing an understanding of organized crime's structures and methods
of operation, the student should be able to gain insights into many
such organizations' strengths and weaknesses, their abilities to
maintain themselves as ongoing organizational units, and their
unique behavioral enforcement techniques.

The most closely examined organized crime group is the
Mafia/La Cosa Nostra. Specific testimonial description of the
internal structure, as well as the philosophy of this group has been
provided by at least two infamous made members: Joseph Valachi
and James Fratianno. Their revelations in the 1960s and 1980s
respectively, coupled with earlier insights,[1] have given investigators and law enforcement officers accurate insights into the heart
of this crime group.

The Mafia's organizational structure is based upon the early
formations of Roman Legions. Joseph Valachi's testimony before

---

[1]"The Death of Petrosino," 46, *Current Literature*, pp. 478–80 (May 1909).

the McClellan Senate Subcommittee in 1963 provided a very thorough description of this structural skeleton of Mafia crime families. His testimony lead to the development of an accurate organizational chart for the Mafia, which was generally disseminated by the President's 1967 Crime Commission in it's *Report*.

The national organization of the Mafia is composed of twenty-four core crime groups,[2] known as "families," which are loosely banded together in a confederation. This Mafia crime confederation is overseen by a commission composed of nine to twelve representatives of the core families. New York City, however, which has five crime families, is always represented on this commission, and these families are considered permanent members of the commission. The other commission representatives are rotated among the other nineteen family crime groups. The commission acts as a judicial, legislative, and executive body. Often, it arbitrates disputes between the families in addition to authorizing assassinations of family heads who have fallen from grace. Smaller councils of families also exist in some cities such as New York, which act as similar intermediate dispute resolving bodies among the various family members in such cities.

The total membership of the La Cosa Nostra is estimated at approximately 5,000 made or initiated members. Although membership has been restricted, limited, and even closed from time to time throughout the group's history, membership must be earned either by the commission of a contract killing or demonstration of other worthy skills; once membership is earned, a formal induction or initiation ceremony must be followed for admission into the group.

The initiation ceremony first revealed publicly by Joseph Valachi involves formal induction following a vote of made members. Once the vote is completed, an oath of fidelity, allegiance and silence is made not upon a Bible but over a .38 caliber revolver and a dagger. The ceremony is conducted by a sophomoric "blood brother" ritual, concluding the induction affair.[3]

---

[2]The President's Crime Commission, The Challenge of Crime in a Free Society: A Report, p. 193 (Washington D.C., 1967).

[3]P. Maas, The Valachi Papers (G. P. Putnam & Sons, New York, 1968).

Perhaps the most important oath of an initiated or made member is the code of silence or "omerta," as it is called, that a member must follow upon pain of death. As a result of this code, only brief and infrequent glimpses have really been provided of La Cosa Nostra's inner-workings over the years.

Each individual family of made members is structured in hierarchical compositional fashion. Family size varies from twenty to 700 members. The family organized crime group is composed of several levels, each insulating the top level from detection and/or prosecution. The family structure is pyramidal in form. At the top or pinnacle is the family leader or *Boss*, often referred to as *Il capo* or *Don*. Below the boss but in an advisory position, without direct staff authority, is an advisor to the boss known as the *Counselor* or *Consigliere*. This position is usually filled by an older and respected family member, whose advice is often solicited on important family matters. Below the boss and in a position of line authority is an *Underboss* or *Sottocapo*. The *Sottocapo* oversees a number of *Lieutenants* or *Caporegima* (sometimes also referred to as *Capodecina*, i.e., "head of ten"), which act as a further buffer between the lowest level of the family, the *Soldiers* or *Soldati*, and the upper echelon members. Each family may have a number of *Caporegimas* who serve as information and order conduits between *Il capo* and the *Soldati*. Often, business partnerships among the *Soldati* members are formed, frequently involving some participation by one of more *Caporegima*.

Most families also have a number of more specialized positions, including most frequently *"Corrupters"* and *"Enforcers."* Although it is not entirely clear where these specialized positions fit within the typical family structure, it is very clear that these positions exist. Members who occupy these positions make significant contributions to the family and its businesses. The *Corrupter* seeks to minimize risk and neutralize government and law enforcement so that business activities can be carried on without interruption. The *Enforcer*, on the other hand, insures that family discipline, the "Omerta," and other aspects of the code of behavior are followed by family members. Upon orders from the top levels of the family structure, the *Enforcer* also arranges for contact killings or assassinations and may on occasion participate in these activities himself.

The exact placement of these specialized positions within a Mafia crime family has not been given by those informers providing glimpses of the organizational structure of the typical Mafia crime family. However, it seems clear that the positions exist within all families regardless of the level where the specialized position actually fits. It may be easier to describe such positions not as positions at all but rather as essential tasks to be performed within the clear hierarchical structure of a Mafia crime family. However, it seems best to recognize the existance of these positions within the total hierarchical structure. It also seems certain that these positions exist in most organized crime groups regardless of ethnic origins.

Aside from these specialized positions, some authorities also contend that other positions, including those occupied by persons known as *Corruptees*, and *Strategists*, exist at least within some Mafia crime families. Although in all families some member must engage in both short– and long-term planning as well as strategic planning (even though no formal position of *Strategist* may exist) the position of *Corruptee* is almost always occupied by a non-family member. That person is generally recruited for assistance from outside the actual family because of his or her position of governmental authority and/or responsibility. Much more infrequently, a made member may be placed in such a position, in which case the *Corruptee* would then be a family member and would probably be much more effective in his work than a non-member *Corruptee*.

The occupancy of such specialized positions may vary with the family and its membership or even current trends. For example, Meyer Lansky, a now deceased Jewish gangster friendly with certain Mafia elements, may have been a top level nonmember *Strategist*. Many families on occasion have had to use outside enforcers to perform actual killings (although the actual assassinations are not typically performed by most family *Enforcers*).

Aside from the typical hierarchical structure of most organized crime Mafia families, lawyers, accountants, and a host of other professionals may also be occupying specialized positions within a family as made members or outside the family as salaried employees. In any case, such specialized positions as well as the positions of

Strategist, Corruptor, Corruptee, and *Enforcer* would seem to be typical for almost all organized crime groups, including certain non-Mafia crime cartels.

The typical Mafia/La Cosa Nostra family is depicted in Figure 2. It should be noted that the specialized positions just discussed may be

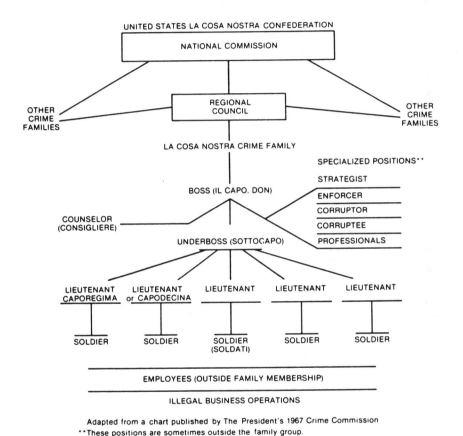

Adapted from a chart published by The President's 1967 Crime Commission
**These positions are sometimes outside the family group.

Revised and reprinted from the President's
1967 Report

Figure 2. La Cosa Nostra organized crime family organizational chart.

outside the family unit or within the family unit, at almost any level.

Although most information has been acquired as to the organizational structure of La Cosa Nostra, other organized crime groups surely follow very similar organizational lines. Some of these groups, moreover, are composed of substantially more members than the actual membership of La Cosa Nostra. For example, there appears to be approximately ten principal Colombian cocaine drug rings in the United States, with total membership approaching 100,000. Typically, each of these rings has members in Colombia, Miami, and New York City. Reportedly, the rings are composed of very able organizers who deal very effectively with Americans.[4]

Regardless of the particular crime group, all organized crime groups are hierarchical in structure, insulating the top levels of the organization from detection and prosecution. Ultimately, the organizations are run in an authoritarian manner with absolute control vested at the top levels of the organization. Often, the individuals seek to mask their true activities or to provide cover for their members through a variety of other business dealings such as certain legitimate business operations or "fronts."

Every organization, in addition, performs a variety of legislative, judicial, and executive functions. In addition, the organizations have perfected, in many instances, insulating techniques that protect their top level positions from accountability for the organization's criminal activities. The persons holding midlevel positions are often mistaken as a consequence of these insulating activities as top level individuals within organizations because such individuals are often the central points for many organizational activities. This mistaken identification is often compounded because of the communication system typically utilized by most organized crime groups. Contrary to most well established orders, organized crime's communication system is almost entirely verbal rather than written so that the risks associated with discovery of written messages are minimized as much as possible. Moreover, verbal messages are usually coded to mask their true meaning, hide identities, and provide vague and ambiguous phrases subject to varying interpretation. The communication process, therefore, makes it very difficult, if not impossible, for many investigators to accu-

---

[4]Andersen, Cate, Jackson, McWhirter, and Simpson, "Crashing on Cocaine," *Time Magazine*, *28* (April 11, 1983).

rately decode the messages and identify higher level persons within any organized crime group.

Most organized crime groups, are held together through the employment of enforcement activities, strict codes of silence, fidelity to the organizational structure, and loyalty among members. Moreover, many of these groups are held together through actual familial or ethnic bonds, further cementing relationships among members of the organization. Membership in such organizations is limited and, in terms of normal society, closed. Often entry into the organization must be earned through some process of loyalty demonstration or performance of a contractual service for the organization (e.g., contract killing, etc.).

Most traditional organized crime groups, principally the Mafia/La Cosa Nostra, have maintained strict codes of behavior so as to limit their own risk of detection and prosecution. Therefore, among the various rules developed principally by the Mafia/La Cosa Nostra, the following are prevalent:

1. Assassinations and violence are limited to members and enemies. The public at large, as well as family members of enemies, are protected from that violence as much as possible;
2. Law enforcement officers are not killed nor are reporters killed or injured; and
3. Loyalty to the organization is paramount to loyalty to true family, God, or Country.

Of late, however, certain emerging groups, including Colombian gangs and the so-called "Black Mafia," as well as other organized crime groups, have deviated from such traditional rules. As a consequence, violence has not been limited to enemies or particular individuals. Often innocent bystanders as well as other noninvolved family members are caught up in the violence.

The methods and weapons used by most organized crime groups to amass and gain power and control over others are not new and have existed for hundreds of years. Machiavelli in his famous work, *The Prince,* succinctly summarized these methods of group control:

1. Violence;
2. Direct in-person dominance; and
3. Protection and payment of tribute.[5]

Organized crime groups have of course, utilized all three methods of control to acquire and maintain power and to accumulate wealth.

As the President's 1967 Crime Commission found in its *Report*, the leaders of organized crime have maintained a strict code of discipline and conduct, which furthers their own needs and which assists them in amassing their power and wealth:

> The code gives the Leaders exploitative authoritarian power over everyone in the organization. Loyalty, honor, respect, absolute obedience — these are inculcated in family members through ritualistic initiation and customs within the organization, through material rewards and through violence ... The code not only preserves leadership authority but also makes it extremely difficult for law enforcement to cultivate informants and maintain them within the organization.[6]

The structure and organizational control maintained by organized crime groups over their memberships as well as the power exercised over the victims upon which they prey has been very effective in assisting organized crime's achievement of its underlying goals of wealth and power acquisition and utilization. As we shall see in upcoming chapters, the structure and philosophy of organized crime has greatly assisted in the development and maintenance of very profitable activities for all organized crime groups.

---

[5]Sommerville and Santoni, *Social and Political Philosophy*, p. 102 (Garden City, New York, Doubleday & Co., 1963).

[6]*Report, supra*, note 2 at 195–6.

Chapter 4

ORGANIZED CRIME ACTIVITIES

Organized crime exists to achieve monetary gain or to obtain enough power to assist in achieving monetary gain. Organized crime figures frequently have demonstrated great skill in attaining this goal. Recent estimates place gross organized crime revenues at between 150 to 200 billion dollars.[1,2] A completely accurate determination of the real gross or net revenues of organized crime is not possible due to the lack of accurate public accounting and recordkeeping. However, there can be little question that it's revenues and net profits are in the billions of dollars. Meyer Lansky, the now deceased former money mover for organized crime, once boasted while referring to organized crime: "We are bigger than U.S. Steel."[3] Today, organized crime is much bigger than U.S. Steel and would certainly exceed the combined incomes of most major United States corporations.

The aftershocks of the acquisition of money of this magnitude are awesome in terms of the power that its use can command. It can be used to dominate legitimate business, to manipulate the stock market, or to elect political candidates to public office. These are all significant and serious threats not only to our economic system but to the very fiber of our democratic system of government.

Internal Revenue Service estimates based upon gross revenues of selected organized crime activities of approximately 65 to 89 billion dollars[4] place net revenues from such operations at

---

[1]Cook, "The Invisible Enterprise," *Forbes Magazine*, p. 60 (September 29, 1980).

[2]Pennsylvania Crime Commission, *A Decade of Organized Crime*: 1980 Report, p. 4 (St. Davids, Pa., 1980).

[3]Cook, *supra*, note 1.

[4]Department of the Treasury, Internal Revenue Service, "Estimates of Income Unreported on Individual Income Tax Returns," Publication 1104, pp. 135–142 (September, 1979).

between 25 to 35 billion dollars.[5] Of this amount, the IRS estimates that *perhaps* as much as 25 percent is reported and taxed by the government. This means that as much as approximately 24 billion dollars escapes any tax imposition whatsoever, and according to other estimates, perhaps as much as 50 billion dollars.[6]

The power that comes with such revenues coupled with other advantages that organized crime has over legitimate business is often staggering to such enterprises. Not only can organized crime escape most tax on its income but it is also essentially free from all laws and regulations because of its illegal methods of operation. It uses those methods and activities in both the underground economic system and the normal economic system as well. The advantages thus given to organized crime over legitimate business often make competition by legitimate business impossible.

Although universal agreement among the authorities is lacking, it appears that drug transactions, gambling, and loansharking are the biggest gross revenue makers for organized crime and in that order.[7] Drug trafficking revenues may be as high as 45 to 63 billion dollars a year, netting perhaps as much as 30 to 45 billion dollars annually, a return of better than 200 percent on initial investments.[8] By far, drug dealings account for the best profit margin and return for organized crime.

Gambling revenues have been consistently high since Prohibition. Although some authorities believe that gambling is the number one gross money maker for organized crime,[9] it does, regardless of its true ranking, bring in perhaps as much as 45 to 56 billion dollars per year.[10] Moreover, it generates a net profit esti-

---

[5]*Id.*

[6]Cook, *supra*, note 1.

[7]*Compare* Cook, *supra*, note 1 with Department of the Treasury, *supra*, note 4, and with PA Crime Commission, *supra*, note 2 at pp. 4–6; and with The Challenge of Crime in a Free Society: A Report By The President's Commission on Law Enforcement and Administration of Justice, pp. 187 to 209 (1967) hereinafter cited as *Report.*

[8]*Id.*

[9]Department of the Treasury, *supra*, note 4.

[10]*Id.*

mated at approximately 10 to 12 billion dollars per year.[11] (The net profit is much lower than that from drug trafficking largely due to the high overhead associated with gambling activities. The risk, of course, is higher with drug transactions but the return is surely higher as well.)

Loansharking activities are often left out of most tables or diagrams of organized crime profits, but such activities must certainly account for at least 20 billion dollars in gross revenues per year.[12] Net profits may be as much as 200 or more percent of the net investment.[13]

Each illegal as well as legitimate enterprise of organized crime exists within a rather loose organizational structure, parts of which directly or indirectly assist in bolstering the other parts. Consumers or customers of one of these units are often referred to or recommended to other units, the referral often necessitated by overindulgence of the consumer in particular activities, i.e., gambling (referral to loan shark).

An examination of each of the major organized crime activities will certainly assist in an overall understanding of the subject. Moreover, the demonstrable interrelationships between the various economic or business units of organized crime can help greatly in gaining insight into the total depth and magnitude of the problems associated with these activities.

Almost all of organized crime businesses involve either direct criminal activity in conducting the business or indirect criminal activity generated as a result of the business itself. For example, unlawful drug transactions often ultimately involve sales to addicts. These addicts, in order to support their habits commit a wide variety of crimes to raise necessary funds for drug transactions. Such activities are the indirect result of the direct crime of drug trafficking and must, at least in part, be attributed to it along with several other related crimes. Each activity of organized crime generally involves crimes of other types which must be examined in order to achieve a truly complete understanding of the problem.

---

[11]*Id.*

[12]Cook, *supra*, note 1.

[13]PA Crime Commission, *supra*, Note 4 at 5–6.

DRUGS

Illicit transactions in drugs by organized crime figures, as we have seen, is one of the mainstays of organized crime profit; perhaps, according to some accounts, the largest gross money maker and, according to most accounts, the largest net income producer. Along with these profits comes some rather significant risks, inasmuch as there is fierce competition among the various organized crime groups for this business. While traditional organized crime factions such as the Mafia/La Cosa Nostra still control a good deal of the world and United States drug trade, other fast growing factions are moving in, particularly on the West Coast and Gulf Coast of the United States as well as in Florida.

Southern Florida has become a battleground among some of these groups including the Mafia and certain Chicano, Cuban, Colombian, and Black groups. The emerging groups do not have as quite a comprehensive code of conduct or behavior as La Cosa Nostra, and as a consequence, warfare has became more risky to anyone even remotely associated with organized crime as well as bystanders and civilians. The Colombians, for example, are reportedly ruthless and capable of extreme acts of violence directed at not only competitors but anyone in the way.[14]

Aside from the open warfare problems, Southern Florida also has become a mecca of sorts for large currency transactions, including an abundance of 20, 50, and 100 dollar bills, drug dealers' main currency commodity. It has been reported that Florida, at times, holds the largest cash currency surplus of the entire United States Federal Reserve System.[15] In all probability this is due to the various monetary transactions flowing from the illegal entry of drugs, principally cocaine and marijuana, into Florida's southern coastline.[16]

Organized crime trafficking in illicit drugs began in earnest

---

[14]Andersen, et al., "Crashing on Cocaine", *Time*, p. 29 (April 11, 1983).

[15]Testimony of Irvin B. Nathan, Deputy Assistant Attorney General, U.S. Department of Justice, before the Senate Permanent Subcommittee on Investigations, December 7, 1979, p. 19, reported in PA Crime Commission, *supra* Note 4 at, 6, Footnote 15. *See also* Cook, *supra*, Note 1.

[16]*Id.*

following Prohibition when the mob's revenues from illegal liquor sales were greatly diminished. The smuggling and related tactics learned during Prohibition would be readily adaptable to drug smuggling along the Eastern and Western Seaboards as well as through Canada and Mexico. Although drug dealing was resisted for a time and perhaps outlawed by some organized crime groups because of the fear that the public's outcry against them would be too strong, thereby increasing the risks associated with dealing, illegal drug trafficking is today a fact of life for almost all organized crime groups. The Mafia or La Cosa Nostra, Chicano and Colombian crime groups, Black Mafia crime groups, motorcycle gangs, as well as others participate to varying degrees in the market. Some groups specialize to an extent in the distribution of certain drugs, e.g., some motorcycle gangs specialize in amphetamines, i.e., "speed," while Colombians specialize in cocaine and marijuana.

Illegal drug traffic in the United States principally involves transactions in heroin, morphine, cocaine, hallucinogenics of all kinds, marijuana, various natural and synthetic drugs, amphetamines, and barbiturates. Although there is not universal agreement among medical authorities, most consider all of these illicit drugs addicting either physically or psychologically or both. Most are capable of causing death due to overdose, and some if mixed with the wrong substances or improperly mixed can cause death by toxic poisoning. Some methods of ingestion for example can also be fatal if accidents occur such as with cocaine "free-basing" (smoking cocaine as it vaporizes in a glass pipe filled with rum or a similar substance). Penalties associated with drug trafficking on both the state and federal level are rather severe. High risks as we have seen, however, produce high profits.

Heroin, an organized crime mainstay, once limited to inner-city slums, is now a countrywide, even a worldwide, problem. Heroin is a product of the opium poppy plant grown in many parts of the world including Turkey, the Golden Triangle Area of Southeast Asia (parts of Burma, Thailand, and Laos), India, Pakistan, Iran, and Afghanistan. Although many of these countries have been in tremendous internal or external upheavals, civil insurrection, and even war, their farmers are continuing to grow the plant just like they have done for centuries from which heroin, morphine, and codeine are produced. In various raw stages, the opium produced from the poppy plant is exported from the producing areas for conversion in clandestine laboratories and then imported into the consuming countries for eventual street sale.

Each section of the distribution chain derives large profits from "cutting" the pure heroin that is imported into the country. Heroin is cut by adding either quinine or milk sugar to it to increase the total volume for sale and to dilute the purity of the heroin itself. The more cuts that occur, the more the heroin is diluted until it reaches its normal street purity of approximately 3 to 5 percent, the remaining volume (95% to 97%) being composed of the cutting substances utilized in the process. Lately, due to fierce competition, heroin has become more pure. Sometimes in today's market a purity of 8 to 9 percent can be found. Tremendous profits are thus derived by the addition of the cutting agent to the pure heroin. In fact, at each level of the process, from farmer to street pusher, tremendous profits are realized. Normally one kilo of morphine base is produced from approximately ten kilos of poppy plant. A kilo of morphine base converts to a kilo of heroin 86 to 96 percent pure. That heroin is then cut down to the point of as low as 3 percent pure heroin. One can see that the cutting process, which increases the volume of the drug while reducing its purity, can convert one kilo of relatively pure heroin (e.g., 96% pure) into 32 kilos of approximately 3 percent pure heroin. Broken down into users' "nickel bags," each containing about 5 grains of cut 3 percent heroin (1 kilo = 35.27 oz. = 15,413 grain = 3,082 nickel bags), the total gross from one kilo of heroin equals over a million dollars, perhaps as much as two million dollars depending upon the price paid for the nickel bag ($10 to $20 per bag). The cutting process, increasing the volume of the heroin while reducing its purity is depicted in Figure 3.

Aside from heroin, organized crime generates substantial revenues from trafficking in cocaine, which is an active alkaloid derived from coca leaves. Cocaine has become the drug of the eighties. Although reportedly nonaddicting, its medical and psychological side effects are significant and frequently disabling.

Cocaine is produced and refined principally in South America. Colombia serves as the source for a good portion of the illegal

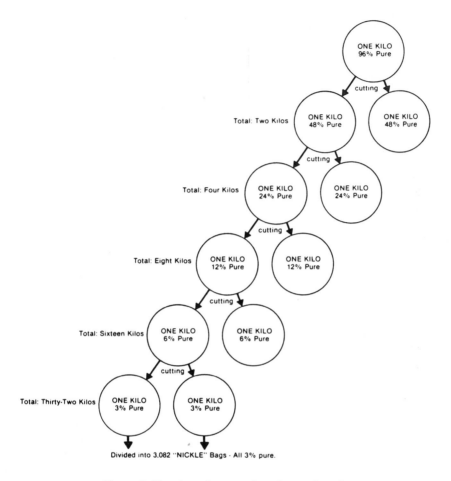

Figure 3. Heroin volume and purity cutting chart.

supply imported into the United States through Florida, other Gulf Coast states, and Mexico, as well as the Eastern Seaboard. Small, twin engine, low flying planes as well as boats or ships of varying sizes typically are used by organized crime to gain illegal entry into the country with this product. Cocaine is cut like heroin, but with vegetable starches or anesthetics such as Novocain.® Typically, it is cut and therefore diluted until it is 15 percent pure. It is sold to consumers by the ounce and may bring as much as $1,000 to $2,000 an ounce or more. The price markup from importation to user is approximately ten times.[17]

Recent successful efforts at curtailing these methods of access into the country, however, have resulted in increased attempts through conventional airplane travel to bring in the cocaine or other drugs through "body packs." By this method, carriers swallow balloons (typically cocaine filled fingers snipped from surgical gloves and tied closed) of the drug or place them in body cavities prior to take off and then after landing remove the balloons or pass them through normal bodily functions. Frequently this method of concealment is successful but highly lethal if the balloons break.

Sometimes heroin and cocaine are utilized together and injected directly into the bloodstream. The process, called "speedballing," reportedly exaggerates the effects of both drugs.

Marijuana and its concentrated derivate hashish were introduced into this country in a rather large way in the late 1950s and 1960s. Widespread use of marijuana and hashish is reported in all literature and in some circles use is considered a normal fact of life. Many organized crime groups import the substance much like cocaine is transferred into the country. Marijuana is more bulky than either cocaine or heroin, and the profits are not as great based upon volume. However, the use is far broader among the populace than either cocaine or heroin and therefore profitable to organized crime.

Enforcement agency efforts to crackdown on the importation of such drugs as marijuana and hashish has contributed to more domestic production of the drugs as "cash crops," especially in the Southwest, California, and Hawaii, which are able to produce a much more potent product than other areas of the country. Distribution systems are widespread and involve many organized crime groups.

Synthetic drugs, barbiturates (called "downers"), and amphetamines (called "uppers") make up the remainder of organized crime's drug product line. Many segments of organized crime participate in this market as well. Much of these items are illegally manufactured within the United States and distributed here or are diverted

---

[17]Andersen, *supra*, Note 14.

from legal markets through various criminal channels into the illegal underground marketplace.

Drug trafficking by organized crime aside from its other effects and costs should demonstrate at least one other chilling attribute: worldwide cooperation among organized crime groups. It would be virtually impossible without a loose-knit confederation of mutual assistance and business dealings for United States organized crime groups to import the various kinds and quantities of drugs into this country.

Although a principal and profitable venture for organized crime, illicit drug trafficking, a series of criminal activities itself (i.e., unlawful drug manufacturing, possession for sale, sale, possession), produces a far reaching series of indirect crimes including murder, assault, robbery, armed robbery, burglary, theft, shoplifting, fencing, receiving and concealing stolen property, insurance fraud, etc. Its costs to society are far reaching and include tax evasion, higher insurance premiums costs, higher costs of certain goods and services due to thefts to support drug habits, loss of economic productivity and profitability due to drug usage, loss of quality control due to drug usage, more job related injuries by workers using such drugs, more public financial assistance for addicts, users, and their families, and public health care costs for drug addicts not to mention the enforcement, prosecution, and judicial costs associated with the criminal justice response to the problem. The total costs certainly exceed the revenues produced from the illicit activity itself.

Profits derived from the activity, like other organized crime activities examined in this chapter, are in substantial part plowed back into the activity as well as other operations of organized crime. In addition, such profits are invested in real estate holdings, legitimate business acquisitions and retention of those businesses, and corruption of public officials, etc. Drug profits in turn create other profits, and money thus begets more money and power.

GAMBLING

Gambling activities for many years were organized crime's largest gross revenue producer. By some accounts, they still are. People have gambled almost from the beginning of time, and many see nothing wrong with the activity at all. Churches, synagogues, schools, charitable organizations, and many states sponsor a variety of gambling activities ranging from Las Vegas style gambling to bingo and lotteries. Often referred to as a "victimless crime," many of its players might be better characterized as willing customers.

Gambling is to be distinguished from many other games. If the outcome of the game is largely determined by chance, it is a gambling activity, while if the outcome is largely determined by skill its probably not such an activity. The outcome of a poker game, for example, although affected to a degree by skill and experience, is largely determined by the chance of the cards being drawn; thus it is a gambling activity. The shooting of a basketball into a basket on the other hand is a skilled activity, and the outcome of that activity is largely determined by skill; hence, it is not gambling. Betting upon certain sporting events, however, is still gambling inasmuch as the outcome of the game between the two teams or players as a betting event is largely determined by chance as to the bettors themselves.

Organized crime activity in this area involves the following:

1. Sports betting;
2. Numbers;
3. Gambling houses, operations, and the like; and
4. Miscellaneous gambling activities.

Sports Betting

Along with the tremendous growth of high school, college, and professional sports in the past twenty years has come an equally large growth in sports betting. Sports betting is controlled for the most part by traditional organized crime families who have joined a loose-knit organization to assist each other in managing sports betting across the country.

Football, basketball, and baseball at all levels is of much interest to the sports-minded gambler. Coupled with boxing and some other sporting contests, the betting adds up to billions of dollars each year and a substantial profit for organized crime.

Sports bets are placed with a "bookmaker" who acts as the bottom tier of a betting network. The bookmaker either in person or over the phone receives the players bets and records them into a "book," frequently using a series of code names for the players to partially disguise the gambling process if it is uncovered. Often when telephone bet placement is used, transfer devices commonly called "black" or "blue boxes" are hooked up to the phones located in empty apartments or motel rooms, which transfer incoming calls from that empty location to another location where the bookmaker remains. These devises are used for the purpose of hampering a trace on the call and the related apprehension of the bookmaker.

The bookmaker also acts as the payoff agent in the event the sports bettor wins and as a collector when a bettor does not. The bet is usually paid after the contest is over. Collection is enforced implicitly and explicitly. Although collection does not proceed to force as fast as with nonpayment to a loan shark, force will be used for collection or to set an example for other sports bettors.

The bookmaker upon the basis of information received from an "odds maker" sets what is called the "line" for sporting contests. Odds makers, who may, at the local level, be the bookmaker himself, typically analyze the teams' past performance and records and then make an educated prediction as to who will win the contest and by how many points. Upon that basis, an allocation of a certain specified number of points to the predicted losing team is made, and thereby the line is set for that game. The line is in essence a point spread designed to make the two teams theoretically equal, so that the chances of either team winning are the same, i.e., one in two. Therefore, the outcome of the game converts from one determined by skill to one determined by chance, and in this context, it is therefore a gambling activity.

Bettors typically put up a specified dollar amount to win an equal amount if their pick is correct. If they win, the bookie therefore pays them an amount equal to the bet. If, however, they lose, they pay the amount of the bet plus an extra 10 percent called "the juice." This 10 percent is the bookmaker's profit, which he gets no matter what the outcome of the contest, so long as he has approximately the same number of bettors on each side of the contest. Often this poses some problems for local bookmakers, and as a consequence, a national bookmaking system has developed to provide a degree of insurance for the bookmaker.

This national bookmaking system is called a "lay-off" system and is used along with adjustments in the line or point spread to ensure the bookmaker's profit. The system works quite easily and effectively. If a bookmaker receives, for example, more bets on his hometown team to win a given sporting contest than he receives for the other team to win, he calls a bookmaker located in the other team's city, an intermediate bookmaker, or a national bookmaker in an effort to lay-off or transfer some of his hometown bets on the hometown team. Often there are bookmakers who specialize in lay-offs and are quite readily available for this purpose. If the local bookmaker is successful in this lay-off, the local bookmaker may agree to take a portion of the other bookmaker's bets so as to even out all bookmaker's bets on either side of a given sporting contest. Thus, both bookmakers hope to achieve an equal balance of bettors on each side. In this event, both bookmaker's risks are reduced to the point of no risk of loss and a clear profit of 10 percent. The process resulting in reduced risk of loss is sometimes referred to as "cover" inasmuch as one bookmaker covers the excess bets of the other and vice versa.

Aside from the lay-off process resulting in a cover for each bookmaker's bets, betting on one side or the other of any sporting contest can be internally encouraged by adjustments to the point spread or line allocated in any given contest. For example, if the hometown team is favored and the other team is given points totalling seven, to make a bet on either, theoretically capable of winning, bets on the other team can be encouraged by increasing the points to eight or nine or ten. In such a manner, in order for a hometown bettor to win on his team, that team would have to win by at least nine or ten or eleven points rather than the original eight points required with a seven point spread (ties lose). As can be seen, an increase or decrease in the point spread can make it harder or easier for any bettor to win in this circumstance, thereby encouraging or discouraging bets on one side or the other of the contest. A bookmaker faced with too many bettors upon a favored hometown team may want, therefore, to increase the point spread or line given to the other team making it more difficult for the hometown team to win, thereby encouraging bets on the other side. In any case, if the bookmaker obtains a balance of bettors through either lay-off or adjustments to the line, he reduced his own risks of loss and ensures his 10 percent profit.

Often in sports betting contests, players have the opportunity to purchase parlay sheets. These sheets permit a variety of contests to be selected in one betting process. Typically, a sheet is obtained or purchased for one dollar, and the player picks three, four, five, or up to ten teams as winners among the sheet options. Point spreads are still used to make the teams theoretically equal and therefore the chances of winning any one contest are still one in two. However, the odds of winning are computed and depicted as follows along with the typical payoff for winning:

Selections	*Odds of Winning*	*Payoff*
3 Teams	1 in 8	$5 for $1 Bet
4 Teams	1 in 16	$9 for $1 Bet
5 Teams	1 in 32	$10 for $1 Bet
10 Teams	1 in 1024	$150 for $1 Bet

The payoff, as can readily be determined, does not even approach the odds of winning with such parlay sheets. The odds of winning are determined as follows:

For each contest with the point spread or line, each team's chances of winning are one chance in two possibilities, or one in two. If two teams must be picked out of two contests, the chances of picking each correctly become more difficult because the pick must be one in two times one in two, or $\frac{1}{2} \times \frac{1}{2}$ or $\frac{1}{4}$—so the odds are one in four of winning. This can be carried out for any number of required picks and the odds keep increasing.

As with regular single contests, parlay sheet contests are sometime adjusted or subjected to lay-off. However, the chances of winning are so slim that the odds compared with the payoffs are definitely in favor of the bookmakers who profit enormously from this activity.

Similar odds distribution systems are used for other sporting contests such as baseball and basketball. With baseball, the odds don't exceed two to one because of the low scores of baseball compared to football or basketball, and the bookmakers juice or profit is generally 20 percent, as it is with most high school sporting contests.

Much concern over the years has been expressed about "fixes" of sporting contests. Some fixes have occurred; however, as a matter of policy, fixes don't benefit the national majority of organized crime. Sports betting operators depend upon the point spread, adjustment to that spread, and lay-offs to equalize the contest, which in turn insures them of their 10 percent profit. While individual gamblers might benefit from a fix or even individual bookmakers or players, by and large the industry of illegal sports betting does not stand to gain but only to lose as a result of such fixes.

Numbers

Organized crime's interest in gambling began with casino gambling during Prohibition and numbers running in inner-city areas. Today, numbers running has continued to flourish, although new organized crime members are taking over the operation, including the emerging Black Mafia and Chicano Mafia groups. This may in part be due to the continued occupancy of inner-city areas by these and other minority groups, traditionally the main players of the numbers game, as well as the upward mobility of certain minority organized crime groups within the organized crime community. It also may be due to the weakening of La Cosa Nostra and the backlash of the Black and Chicano underlings heretofore used in low level positions within the Mafia's numbers racket empire. Jealousies as a result of "outsiders" profiting from inner-city people often leads to this takeover by the underlings already familiar with the operations.

Numbers operators despite their small per bet dollar volume, which is typically 25 cents or less to several dollars, generate very significant gross dollar volumes and net profits. In a numbers game, a player selects a number, most often either 0 to 999 in a three-digit system or 0 to 99 in a two-digit system. After selection of the number, which is written down and the bet placed, a fix-proof, predetermined method utilized for the selection of the winning number is monitored each day, and if the bettor's number is selected, he wins. The results of daily horse races or even daily stock market quotations are used as the means of determining the daily winning number. The payoff is typically $600 for each dollar bet in a three-digit system (with the odds of winning set at 1 in 1,000 since there are 1,000 possible combinations from 0 to 999) or $60 for each dollar bet in a two-digit system (with the odds of winning set at 1 in 100 since there are 100 possible combinations from 0 to 99). Sometimes, bettors must risk more than they can win to provide the profit to the numbers operator.

Typically, a numbers operation is run by a given organized crime group that maintains the "bank" or the money behind the operation. The bank finances the operation, pays the winners, and oversees those working for the operation. Below the bank, a series of "controllers" or middle management people hire and oversee the work of the next level manned by "collectors" who move from location to location collecting numbers bets or maintain a standing location where bettors come to place the bets. Bets are placed on sheets called "receipts" or "markers" and then transported by the collectors back to the controllers for ultimate transmission to the bank at the end of each day's work.

Collectors and controllers each receive a commission of all bets placed by them or through their respective "offices." Normally, the collector receives a commission of 25 percent of all bets while the controller receives a commission of 10 percent on all bets placed through his office. Collectors also typically take a percentage of any winner's receipts.

Numbers operators in large cities can employ thousands of people. Millions in annual profits can be generated from a large city numbers operation. Although such operations prey primarily upon the inner-city poor, such gambling activities have expanded to a small degree to the suburbs. This shift will probably continue as long as profits are generated.

Funds generated by numbers operations, as with drug profits, are plowed back into the system and other lucrative organized crime activities as well as legitimate businesses. Annual profits are surely in the billions.

As partially discussed in Chapter 8, the state response to gambling, particularly the numbers game, has typically been to provide a legalized alternative. Thus in some states, churches, charities, nonprofit associations and the state have to one degree or another entered the marketplace with at least two hopes: to raise funds for state use and as a consequence divert money from illegal enterprises thereby adversely affecting those enterprises. Such latter hopes have not really been achieved for several principal reasons: first, winnings received from such legitimate operations are reported to taxing authorities and are therefore taxed; second, the minimum bet is often a dollar or more, which many in the inner city cannot afford; and third, the odds of winning are not as good and the amount paid out is not as much as with illegal operations. Such competition to drive organized crime out of this business is not, therefore, effective. In fact, it may increase participation and interest in gambling generally, therefore contributing to organized crime gambling revenues and profits.

Gambling Houses and Operations

One of the earliest and most traditional gambling enterprises for organized crime has been the gambling house, where players behind locked and sometimes reinforced doors are given the opportunity to play a variety of casino games including craps, roulette, kino, poker, black jack, and the like. The "house," sometimes referred to as a private club (often under the misguided notion that that label created a lawful operation), often takes a percentage of each pot or play won by their bettors in various games. Food, drink, and sometimes related entertainment, e.g., prostitutes, are provided or available.

Such houses and operations flourish all across the country and have for many years. Although local law enforcement agencies frequently raid such operations, they often move from place to place several times a year. Total profits from these illicit operations, (outside of Nevada or Atlantic City) certainly are in the millions. Profits again are reinvested in all of organized crime's activities.

Miscellaneous Gambling Activities

Organized crime also has invested in a variety of other gambling ventures, some of which are illegal off-track horse race betting, which may in fact be more profitable than numbers operations, dog racing, cock fighting, and dog fighting. Illegal off-track horse betting, once extremely popular, still accounts for millions in profits for organized crime. Efforts in New York to establish legitimate off-track horse betting stations may have affected illegal organized crime operations but only to a degree due to the same problems that arise from efforts to legalize certain gambling activities.

Dog and cock fighting, particularly gruesome activities, put animals in fight to the death contests, the results of which are the subject of much betting. Small organized crime groups generally run these operations. Profits from these activities would, of course, be among the smallest of organized crime's gambling ventures.

Organized crime is also involved in the distribution of all sorts of gambling paraphernalia used for the most part in its illegal gambling houses and often under the guise of charitable operations. These would include a wide variety of games, instant winner variety gambling tickets, and lottery materials.

Organized crime's involvement in legitimate gambling in Las Vegas, Nevada, and Atlantic City, New Jersey, locations, as well as other locations around the world, has been readily documented. The enormous sums generated by such establishments are often skimmed of millions upon millions of dollars, all of which wind up in organized crime coffers for a variety of uses. Most people gamble or approve of gambling[18] despite strong recommendations against gambling.[19]

The direct crimes of gambling relate principally to the activity itself and are generally classified as gambling, promoting gambling, maintaining a place for gambling, and the like. The indirect crimes resulting from gambling as well as the indirect social and economic consequences are perhaps the most serious and disturbing problem. Gamblers unable to repay gambling debts often turn to loan sharks for monies to repay their wagering debts and thereby get in deeper and deeper. Frequently, they turn to criminal activities to repay their debts.

---

[18]Presidential Commission on the Review of a National Policy Toward Gambling, *Gambling in America*, 1 (1976).

[19]Report, *supra*, Note 7 at 188.

Loansharking

Loansharking, like the two preceding organized crime activities, is a major money maker for organized crime, generating perhaps as much as 20 billion dollars a year in revenues.[20] It has been and continues to be a major enterprise of organized crime. Its most significant threat, however, does not stem from its obvious activities but rather from its subtle uses in business takeovers, bankruptcy scams, burglaries and burglary scams, insurance frauds, and arson.

Loansharking, also known as "shylocking," is the lending of money at exorbitant interest rates (usury), the repayment of which is enforced with violence and threats of violence. Some have suggested that one's body really serves as collateral for such loans,[21] and that is probably a true characterization for the process.

Although the "shark" will, if necessary, use force or even kill, his major concern is the perpetuation of interest income, or as it is called in the business "vigorish." Repayment of principal is not important when the interest rates are as high as 2000 percent per year.

The traditional loansharking arrangement will require repayment of $6.00 in principal and interest for each $5.00 borrowed at the end of one week. This converts to a 20 percent interest rate per week or 1040 percent per year ($6.00 − $5.00 = $1.00; $1.00 ÷ $5.00 = 20% × 52 weeks = 1040%). This rate, however, often varies and may go as high as 2000 percent coupled with late charges, "penalties," and the like.

Loansharking operations typically are run by a hierarchical three-tier structure with the financier or operation boss at the top and with middle management and lower sharks below him. The cut between the three tiers provides a 1 percent per week return to the boss (52% per year) and a 1.5 percent to 2.5 percent per week payment of interest to middle management. In such a loansharking system, middle management also lends out a much larger dollar amount than the lower level sharks. Enforcers are used at these

---

[20]Cook, *supra*, Note 1.

[21]PA Crime Commission, *supra*, Note 2 at 156.

two levels, if necessary, to compel payment and to "set up" slow or nonpayers as examples to others.

Customers of loan sharks often turn to the sharks in times of financial desperation. Soon they learn that their status as customers or clients changes to that of victims. If they cannot continue paying the vigorish, they face serious risks personally and to their families. Often the shark suggests ways out to his desperate client; frequently those suggestions are taken up.

These suggestions include the following:

1. *Transmittal of favors for loan or interest forgiveness.* These favors run the full gamut. Mill workers are sometimes asked to assist in shark operations, leave doors or windows open for easy nighttime access, or smuggle out of the mill certain parts, plans, machinery or tools; security guards are asked to "look the other way" during burglaries or to provide alarm plans, security plans, access to buildings, valuables, locations, or travel routes. Home security alarm system installers are asked for access plans, alarm bypass mechanisms, and lists of customers with valuable possessions; businessmen may be asked for their product or for a source to sell other products produced or obtained by the shark or access to the plant workers for gambling or drugs or access for food or vending machines; dentists, doctors, or druggists may be asked for drugs or prescriptions or the like. The list is really unending and as long as the occupations served by a loan shark.

2. *Sharing of customer's businesses.* This is one of the favorites of most sharks with customers who can no longer pay interest. The shark offers a forgiveness of debt or interest for a percentage of the customer's business, often as a "silent partner." When this happens, the customer is often left with nothing and some impossible explaining to do. The scenario usually follows a set path. After a time as a silent partner, a decision is made to order stock on credit; this may go on gradually for several months with suppliers who initially receive prompt payment, then a much larger order is placed, delivered, and billed, and the merchandise is surreptitiously removed. A burglary is then staged or arson committed, and the insur-

ance proceeds are paid for the loss with full participation by the shark in those proceeds. Since the merchandise "loss" is blamed upon burglars or the fire, insurance payment is made for that loss as well. The supplier, however, is not paid, and the shark not only has the merchandise that he has diverted from the store or the business but also the money from the insurance company for the "loss" as well. The shark then gracefully exits, often leaving the business with no choice but bankruptcy.

Similar arrangements are often followed as to several or many different suppliers; the goods are received and the shark backs out and leaves the customer to file bankruptcy. Various twists on the same basic theme are committed each day. They cannot only involve supplies and insurance companies but also banking institutions, pension funds, employee benefit plans, and the like.

3. *Commission of crime.* Often a customer unable to pay will be forced to commit criminal acts to repay or for the benefit of the shark. The list of criminal acts is also endless and the only limitation is one's imagination. Frequently, however,the customer will be asked to make certain deliveries of contraband or to commit theft crimes or the like. Customers such as stockbrokers, bankers, insurance executives, or pension and/or employee fund managers have access to a great deal of funds, many of which can be tapped for the benefit of the shark.

Loan sharks will even lend to other criminals and their enterprises often at somewhat reduced but still usurious interest rates. Disputes regarding such loans are generally decided among "arbitration" panels within organized crime rather than by force. Loansharking results in some rather heinous direct criminal activity, largely as a result of payment enforcement, e.g., assault, battery, attempted murder, kidnapping, and murder in addition to criminal usury. Indirectly, the activity results in far greater monetary crime: tax evasion, robbery, theft, embezzlement, fraud, arson, bankruptcy scams, etc. The use of loansharking as a means to gain access to legitimate business is perhaps the crimes most serious threat to society.

THEFTS, FENCING AND COMPUTER THEFTS

Organized crimes' involvement in theft and fencing activities is well documented. Annual gross income for such activities runs into the hundreds of millions of dollars, perhaps more. Theft and fencing activities are natural by-products of organized crime's three main income producing activities as well as other less lucrative pursuits. Such activities occur every day, in fact every hour of the day.

Some authorities have theorized that professional criminal activity could not exist without two essential relationships within legitimate society of which fencing is one. Fencing provides a ready bounty for the thief who can peddle his wares with some ease, and in most cases with relatively low risk.

Not much is known of fencing per se, which may be defined as the surreptitious purchase and sale of illegally obtained goods within the underground economic system. Professional thieves and fences, despite some lack of knowledge as to the latter, work in a state of mutual cooperation, a symbiotic relationship of sorts. That relationship is not established by formal contracts or the like but rather is founded upon supply and demand factors cemented by trust as well as fear. The theft and fencing activities of organized crime are boundless and include the following:

1. Securities thefts;
2. Embezzlements;
3. Hijacking and cargo thefts;
4. Cargo pilferage;
5. Large-scale cigarette, alcohol, and beer thefts;
6. Thefts committed during burglaries and breaking and enterings;
7. Bank and other financial institution robberies;
8. Auto and other vehicular thefts;
9. Auto and other vehicular parts thefts;
10. Thefts of merchandise and other goods of all kinds; and
11. Fencing of all of the above.

The theft of certain of the goods listed above often leads to and greatly contributes to further costly crime. Security thefts, for example, even those obtained in burglaries, can often readily be used as security for loans from banks or other financial institutions. As we discuss later in this chapter, such loans can quite readily result in thousands of dollars lost, which when computed all across the country and, in fact, all over the world, can result in millions lost.

Thefts of nonpersonally usable goods other than items with inherent instrinsic value would soon cease without a fencing distribution network. Moreover, the significant cash flow required of an addict or user, gambler, or loan shark customer often encourages thefts from which fencing activities necessarily flow to provide the means to raise the needed funds.

As we will discuss in Chapter 5, organized crime keeps up with technological advances to foster its goals and profits. Technological improvements in the reproduction of records, tapes, video tapes, and movies have lead to the development of a whole new organized crime industry: record, tape, video, and film piracy. Such entertainment items are purchased legitimately, illegally reproduced, packaged with counterfeit labels and covers, and then sold as genuine articles. Millions are thus siphoned from legitimate producers and copyright holders of such artistic productions.

Continued growth of computerized information storage and retrieval systems has resulted in organized crime's increasing involvement in computer theft and related activities. Access to most computer systems, be it a credit card system, merchandise ordering system, or the like, requires input of coded information that acts much like a combination lock, i.e., without the proper combination given in the proper sequence, no access to the system can be obtained. Many such computer access codes are easily broken, often through the use of other computers. Once the code is obtained, access through a computer terminal attached through a communication line, e.g., a telephone line, can readily be obtained. Once hooked up to the computer, the information thereby obtained can sometimes be manipulated to issue credit cards, extend lines of credit, transfer funds or securities from account to account, order merchandise, determine security systems or security routes, issue credits to existing accounts, learn of loans extended to businesses or individuals, obtain customer lists and profit information, learn of business trade secrets, formulas, or processes, and learn of an individual's bank deposits and assets, marital history, and health records.

The valuable information that can thus be obtained is almost limitless. More and more information thus transferred into computer storage is subject to retrieval by organized crime. Often, illegal access is not even known in such situations until long after the fact or perhaps never.

INFILTRATION INTO LEGITIMATE BUSINESS, FRAUDS, SCAMS, BANKRUPTCY, AND ARSON

Perhaps more than any other enterprise, the use of a variety of tactics, most either fraudulent or coercive, to gain a foothold into the legitimate business community is of increasing and serious concern. Organized crimes' interest in such acquisitions are several-fold. As the President's Crime Commission found in its *Report*:

> To have a legitimate business enables the racket executive to acquire respectability in the community and to establish a source of funds that appears legal and upon which just enough taxes can be paid to avoid income tax prosecution.[22]

Organized crime's involvement in this area has been particularly disturbing to some in the business community itself. The U.S. Chamber of Commerce stated in 1970:

> Practically every type of business and industry in the United States is currently being exploited or penetrated by an awesome, powerful, and no-holds barred competitor—a conglomerate of crime. This criminal conglomerate employs thousands, nets billions annually, operates nationwide and internationally, possesses an efficient and disciplined organizational structure, wields a depressingly effective lobbying apparatus, insulates itself against legal action, hurts billion dollar corporations and cripples smaller companies, and, according to many, rates as the most serious long-term danger to the security and principles of this nation.[23]

---

[22]Report, *supra*, Note 7 at 189–190.

[23]Chamber of Commerce of the United States, *Deskbook on Organized Crime*, p. 3 (1970).

Although the President's Crime Commission found some evidence in 1967 of a "lack of interest" on the part of some legitimate businesses as to with whom they deal,[24] there is a growing awareness of the enormous and severe consequences of the problem. Estimates have been put forth indicating that about 10,000 legitimate businesses are owned by organized crime groups, deriving profits of perhaps 12 billion dollars each year.[25] Certain legitimate businesses are of special interest to organized crime groups and individuals. Some of these are coin operated-vending machine business, garment business, bars, restaurants, taverns, hotels and motels, cheese, olive and other foodstuff businesses, laundries and other cleaning entities, automobile agencies, trucking companies, waterfront activities, bakeries, entertainment companies, and dumps and refuse services. Such business enterprises heretofore selected by organized crime have been so targeted because of the ability to funnel funds (i.e., launder illegally obtained money) through such largely cash businesses. In addition, organized crime members can obtain an air of respectability and employability through such legitimate employment and also obtain thereby a means of reporting a portion of their illegally derived income for tax purposes. Other unfair and illegal tactics and methods certainly give organized crime a substantial edge over legitimate business.[26]

Strong-arm tactics can be used in many ways to gain competitive edges for mob controlled or operated businesses. Monopolies of sorts, for example, for the purchase of goods and services, can thus be created. Moreover, such businesses can often employ illegal aliens brought into the country for a "contract price," then hire and employ such persons at salaries below minimum wage, without regard to income tax, social security, or other withholdings and without compliance as to employee health or safety laws. Some legitimate business ventures of organized crime acquired as an indirect result of illegal enterprises or established as a front for fraudulent purposes can often be used to obtain fraudulent loans, insurance loss payments, and the like. "Control of business con-

---

[24]Report, *supra*, Note 7 at 198.

[25]PA Crime Commission, *supra*, Note 2 at 214.

[26]Report, *supra* Note, 7 at 190.

cerns has usually been acquired through one of four methods: (1) investing concealed profits acquired from gambling and other illegal activities; (2) accepting business interest in payment of the owner's gambling debts; (3) foreclosing on usurious loans; and (4) using various forms of extortion."[27]

Such tactics have been used to gain control of brokerage houses, savings and loans, meatpacking firms, and a myriad of other business establishments. The profitability of such ventures and the added benefits flowing into organized crime coffers as a result of ownership of such institutions foretells of greater, future organized crime involvement in this area. The costs generated by such infiltration are very difficult to assess. Clearly the following economic consequences frequently arise from organized crime's infiltration into legitimate business: legitimate business is driven out of the marketplace because of an inability to compete; inferior and sometimes defective, adulterated, or harmful products are sold at highly inflated prices; certain monopolies are created; tax dollars are lost; insurance premiums due to frauds or scams are increased; and costs of all affected goods and services rise.

Often such businesses are within the tentacles of organized crime as silent partners. They are often used in one of the following manners to generate additional funds:

Bankruptcy Scams

A business is "taken over" by one of several previously described methods. Business for a time continues as usual and gradually orders are placed for goods on established credit. Once the goods are received they are quickly sold or diverted to other channels. The cash generated thereby is diverted to other activities of organized crime and the business is then put into bankruptcy.

Arson/Burglary Scams

A business is "taken over" as above described. Orders for goods are placed on credit, the goods are sold, the cash diverted, and either an arson or burglary is staged. Insurance proceeds for the cost of goods are then collected and often diverted, usually without

---

[27]*Id*

payment to the supplier. Frequently, the firm is then forced into bankruptcy.

Fraud

Often, a business taken over by organized crime can be used to commit large-scale swindles in land deals, securities, home improvements, credit card losses, and the like. For example, an organized crime member can open a clothing store, stock merchandise, establish a credit card charge privilege for its customers and then have other organized crime members come in, buy stock, and make purchases on stolen credit cards.

Afterwards, the goods so obtained are quickly and easily sold. Often, credit cards can quite readily be used for a time before the loss is even reported or made known to the merchant. In this manner, the store operator would remain free of suspicion. Insurance is also often available to cover such "losses."

The total cumulative effect of organized crime's continuing involvement and interest in legitimate business has yet to be assessed. It is without question a grave danger to our economic and political system.

LABOR RACKETEERING

Organized crime's involvement in labor racketeering is also quite well established.[28] Although organized crime's access to labor unions was originally gained some years ago, when union organizational activities first began and organized crime "muscle" was needed to counter employer violence, modern organized crime interest in union activities centers primarily upon the use of the labor unions for specific purposes:

1. Access to union pension, welfare, trust, and employee benefit plans in the form of loans to organized crime fronted groups, consulting fees, health, life, and other insurance contracts, payouts of all kinds from those funds, and certain other similar shams.

---

[28]*Id.*

2. Use of labor union members to assist in certain organized crime enterprises such as hijacking, cargo thefts, cargo pilferage, and the like.
3. Use of labor unions to achieve so-called sweetheart contracts with management in return for a variety of favors from management such as access to the factories and offices of the company for gambling, loansharking, and similar organized crime activities, as well as other benefits such as direct payments to organized crime members, "jobs" for organized crime members, products for organized crime members, and the like.
4. Use of labor unions to drive out of business certain competition of organized crime controlled legitimate enterprises by encouragement of walk outs, strikes, grievances, and the like.
5. Use of labor unions to extract "labor relations" or "labor consulting" fees from construction companies or contractors intent upon completing projects while unions are told to slow down or stop work. Once payment is made, work progresses as usual, and the building project is completed.

Millions upon millions of dollars have been siphoned from union member benefit funds for worthless or near worthless loans for organized crime members or their fronted organizations. Typically, loans are granted by organized crime controlled boards of trustees with no security or greatly overvalued security to dummy corporations formed as fronts for organized crime. When the loan goes bad, the security vanishes or is not worth nearly the amount of the loan, the corporation goes bankrupt, and the union members are really left holding the bag.

The Teamsters Union, among others, has been under intense scrutiny for years because of such activities and tactics. Recent efforts to stop such practices have resulted in replacement of union trustees with professional insurance money managers to care for the welfare and pension funds of the Teamsters. Whether or not such devices will curb fraudulent or worthlessly secured loans remains to be seen. Millions of dollars has also paid out to consultants or agents fronting for organized crime interests, which often obtain lucrative contracts for certain specified services for unions and their members such as medical care insurance.[29]

CORRUPTION OF PUBLIC OFFICIALS

Organized crime cannot exist without corruption of governmental employees including law enforcement officers, prosecutors, judges, and penal system personnel.[30] Corruption of such persons serves organized crime's objectives of making money and profit,[31] negates and nullifies governmental interference,[32] and reduces the risks of doing business.[33] Corruption takes many forms and often extends over many years. For example, organized crime will often provide funds and expertise to young aspiring politicians seeking public office in the hopes of future pay back if they are elected to that of some other public office.[34]

Opportunities to corrupt, aside from the most obvious (i.e., money payments either directly or indirectly to political campaign committees, corporations, charities, etc.), often arise out of the very human weaknesses that organized crime normally manipulates in its varied business activities. For example, politicians, police, legislators, judges, and bureaucrats are all in many respects representative of the population as a whole. Some of these individuals have vices just like everyone else. These vices may be personal or they may be vices of a close friend or family member. The vice may be gambling, drugs, or sexual perversions or needs. The list can be as long as corresponding human weaknesses. Since organized crime is in business to supply such services to meet most needs, it is easy for organized crime to use those services to grant and then extract favors and thereby corrupt the politician or

---

[29]*Id.* at 190–1.

[30]*Id.* at 191.

[31]National Advisory Committee on Criminal Justice Standards and Goals, Task Force on Organized Crime, *Organized Crime*, p. 23 (1976).

[32]*Id.* at 24.

[33]*Id.* at 29.

[34]M. Haller, "Organized Crime in Urban Society: Chicago in the Twentieth Century," p. 35 Journal of Social Issues *88* (1979).

governmental servant. Blackmail and extortion are often the main-stays utilized to ensure compliance with organized crime requests for favors.

The favors extracted from organized crime corruption through its activities are used to foster and further organized crime goals, such as the following:

1. Nonenforcement of penal laws;
2. Nonenforcement or lax enforcement of building codes, fire codes, safety codes, and similar laws or local ordinances;
3. The granting of certain desired permits, licenses, or zoning variances;
4. The granting of governmental contracts and the provisions of goods and services to governmental entities;
5. Dismissal of criminal charges or liberal plea bargaining; and
6. Light sentencing or the granting of probation or parole.

Corruption results in a perversion of the political process and is harmful to all segments of society. It undermines the government, exposes its citizens to danger, increases costs, and ultimately destroys confidence in government.

MISCELLANEOUS ORGANIZED CRIME ACTIVITIES

The foregoing discussion of organized crime activities is not all-inclusive. There are a wide variety of other crimes practiced by organized crime groups, all of which benefit to one degree or another the total criminal enterprise. These are the five most prevalent:

1. *Prostitution*. Although not as large scale as it once was, which may be due in part to a change in public mores, prostitution still flourishes. Revenues from such transactions probably exceed one billion dollars per year.[35]
2. *Pornography.* The 1970s saw a dramatic increase in and a somewhat more public demand for this product. Organized crime, long in the forefront of pornography, stepped in to fill the demand. More exotic examples of pornography supplied by organized crime include child pornography,

---

[35]PA Crime Commission, *supra*, Note 2 at 5.

rape scenes, and actual sex murders on film.

3. *Illegal Cigarette or Liquor Sales.* To a degree, organized crime utilizes many of the legitimate business enterprises to sell such illegally obtained products in a variety of ways, often without payment of excise or related taxes.

4. *Importation of Illegal Aliens.* Various organized crime groups regularly assist in the smuggling of aliens into this country. For the most part, these aliens are simply looking for work and usually pay for organized crime's efforts to bring them into the country. Sometimes, they are committed to extended periods of servitude as part of the deal. Often, they are used in various organized crime enterprises including restaurants, laundries, garment manufacturing establishments, and factories. The profits derived from such enterprises can be very large. For example, one recently uncovered alien smuggling ring in New Mexico grossed more than 24 million dollars annually, more than half being profit.[36]

5. *Counterfeiting.* Organized crime's involvement in this activity goes back many years. It includes efforts to counterfeit currency, securities of all kinds, negotiable instruments, letters of credit, credit cards, government documents, and many other similar papers. The latest in technological advances are utilized by organized crime often with great success.

THE BIG PICTURE

Organized crime's various activities and enterprises represent an "invisible"[37] business conglomeration. The conglomeration is held together through loose-knit contacts, familial relationships, necessities of doing business, and the interdependence of certain activities, those activities causing certain symbiotic relationships to develop. The "big picture" of organized crime ventures, businesses, enterprises, and activities would be enough to make any worldwide conglomerate jealous. The profits of organized crime are plowed back into the system, used to generate more

---

[36]*Canton Repository*, "Whats Happening," p. 1, June 24, 1982.

[37]Cook, *supra*, Note 1.

money in a self-perpetuating evil enterprise, preying upon the weak, rewarding the strong and vicious, and costing everyone harm and money in the process. Money, power, fear, and corruption are the mortar that holds the whole together.[38]

Analysis of the big picture of organized crime, summarizing of its enterprises and tracing of its cash flow, may be accomplished by diagramming organized crime's three main activities, showing the interrelationships of those activities to its other activities, and tracing the flow of money through those various business ventures (see Figure 4).

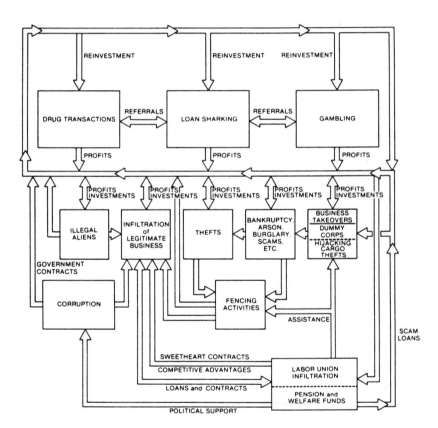

Figure 4. Organized crime cash flow, investment, reinvestment, and activities.

---

[38]*Report, supra*, Note 7, at 189–191.

Perhaps the entire enterprise was best summarized by Los Angeles County, California Sheriff Peter J. Pitchess as follows:

> The actions of organized crime are rarely compulsive, but are the products of intricate conspiracies carried out over long periods of time aimed at gaining control over entire fields of activity for the express purpose of amassing tremendous sums of money. Every time we buy a can of peas, a television set, a shirt, cheese — every time we buy beer, wine, liquor, a bar of soap, perfume, luggage, meat or almost anything we pay a tribute to the crime syndicate, and don't you forget it. Wherever organized crime has gotten a foothold it has never been broken historically. Never. You have never eliminated it from any community where it ever once got a foothold.[39]

---

[39]Cook, *supra*, Note 1 at 71.

Chapter 5

CONTEMPORARY ORGANIZED
CRIME TRENDS

As with any social structure, organized crime has undergone and is presently undergoing some dramatic changes. Many of these changes have not as yet been completed and may never be due to the evolutionary, self-perpetuating nature of organized crime. The outcome of this evolutionary process is in some respects uncertain, inasmuch as the end result is to be determined by force, intimidation, and cunning. Some of these changes are merely repetitive rises and falls of various individual personalities in certain organized crime groups. For example, in the 1970s and so far in the 1980s, significant changes have taken place at the top levels of the United States La Cosa Nostra crime families. Mafia family crime leaders in many U.S. cities have either been convicted of various crimes or are awaiting trial. Others have either been executed or died of natural causes.[1]

Aside from the inevitable rise and fall of individual organized crime personalities, other more significant changes have been and are now taking place. To fully appreciate these changes, a review of certain historical processes is of some significance. In Chapter 2, we explained the historical development of organized crime. In the United States, organized crime groups developed from the mass of immigrants swelling our shores between the late 1800s and the early 1900s. From these various ethnic groups, several spawned large and powerful organized crime groups that changed from time to time as each new wave of immigrants was assimilated into society. Organized criminal activity became a sort of "queer ladder

---

[1]Cook, "The Invisible Enterprise," *Forbes Magazine*, p. 60 (September 29, 1980).

of social mobility"[2] allowing immigrants to step up from their often lowly status upon arrival in the United States.

This "ethnic succession"[3] among organized crime groups commenced as the first powerful American immigrant organized crime group, Irish gangs, began to amass significant profits and political power as a result of their illicit operations. As they developed more legitimacy, they were gradually succeeded by Jewish gangs, who for the most part were quickly assimilated into the mainstream of American society. Following the Jews, the Italians and Sicilians began to move up and were jettisoned into power by the end of Prohibition in 1933. This latter group continues to maintain a very powerful profile even today. However, as we shall see, that power may be ebbing away as the evolutionary ethnic succession process continues.

By 1931, the Mafia had approximately 5000 formally inducted members. Soon thereafter, membership was closed until 1954 when formal Mafia induction began again. As a practical consequence of approximately twenty years with no new inductions, the Mafia's membership stagnated at its 1931 level of approximately 5,000 members divided among twenty-four core groups or crime families. Today many of the pre-1931 members are aged and under intense prosecutorial scrutiny. The offspring and grandchildren of these members have had a much softer life in many respects than their forefathers. They are better educated, more respectable, and more readily absorbed into mainstream American society. Reportedly, these generations are not as tough or as willing to dirty their own hands with business or enforcement problems. This second and third generation weakness, coupled with the greater absorbtion of Italian-Americans and Sicilian-Americans into our society, as well as the advancing age and increased prosecution of the older generation members, has definitely hurt the Mafia and its organized activities. In addition, contemporary federal and state prosecutors, utilizing agent infiltration techniques, and grants of immunity for Mafia members turned states' witnesses have exposed the inner-

---

[2]Bell, "The Myth of the Cosa Nostra", *46, The New Leader*, p. 12–15 (December 23, 1963).

[3]F. Ianni, *Ethnic Succession in Organized Crime, Summary Report 1* (U.S. Dept. of Justice, Washington, D.C., 1973).

workings of the Mafia to public, legislative, and prosecutorial scrutiny.

The end result of all of these processes has weakened La Cosa Nostra. Some have proclaimed of late that the Mafia in certain geographical areas has been "decimated," while others have simply concluded that these factors have all put the Mafia "under the gun."[4] However, the Mafia's biggest threat probably will come from within the organized crime structure itself as a continuing result of the process of ethnic succession with very definite accompanying risks to all of society.

Today, new immigrants to the United States, some illegal aliens and resident aliens, as well as certain segments of American minorities are moving into areas and enterprises traditionally controlled by the Mafia. Puerto Ricans, Mexicans, Colombians, Cubans, Chinese, Koreans, Japanese, and Israelis as well as Black and other American-born minorities are all ready, willing, and able to complete, by force if necessary, transitions to power. Some of this evolutionary process is already taking place, often with frightening consequences. It is in many respects similar to the Mafia's own rise to power and succession from the turn-of-the-century Jewish and Irish organized crime gangs that we discussed in Chapter 2.

The Mafia, as we examined in Chapters 2 and 3, has certain codes of behavior. Generally, their violence is limited to themselves. For example, La Cosa Nostra has rules against killing policemen and reporters and has historically limited its violence to its own ranks, while scrupulously protecting even an enemy's family and children.[5] Today, however, such rules have very little meaning to the new emerging crime groups. Gangland wars in Florida, the Pacific Northwest, California, and elsewhere have all affected and hurt otherwise innocent persons. There clearly seems to be a greater willingness in the new groups to use deadly force indiscriminately and more readily at any necessary opposing target to achieve their own purposes. The Colombian crime groups, for example, have been quite ominously characterized: "They're

[4]"Guilty Verdicts 'Decimate' Cleveland Mafia," *The Repository* (Associated Press, Saturday, July 10, 1982, p. 2, col. 3).

[5]T. Plate, *The Mafia at War*, p. 4–5 (N.Y. Magazine Press, 1972).

absolutely ruthless, and they've imported their way of doing business to this country. . . . Heroin dealers in Harlem didn't wipe out each other's whole families. They did-in one guy on a bar stool . . . The Colombians wipe out the whole bar."[6]

Such wholesale violence is not limited to the Colombians. There have been reports, for example, that other emerging organized crime groups such as certain motorcycle gangs have been amassing and stockpiling weapons for an upcoming "biker's war."[7] The so-called "Israeli Mafia" (composed of recent Israeli immigrants to the U.S., many of whom are ex-cons and former military commandos) has also demonstrated particularly debased savagery, reportedly dismembering some of its victims.[8] The Yakuza, or Japanese Mafia, another emerging ethnic crime group composed of ethnic Japanese-Americans (whose original homeland is also not free from organized crime)[9] also uses similarly debased and violent methods to further its own purposes (e.g., threatening to cut off a kidnapped child's fingers if a gambling debt was not paid by the child's father).[10] These increasingly violent tactics pose risks to all of society.

The emerging groups increased willingness to use indiscriminate force has posed rather significant and obvious problems for the Mafia, especially in drug trafficking where the transition from old to new is the most obvious as well as the most potentially lucrative to the new groups. There is little the Mafia can do to change the course of events or coming onslaught. One respected commentator has summed up the problem: "The Mafia is self-destructing. It's lost muscle and power, and now it has a lot of competition from the new guys on the block. . . . They've moved in, especially in the drug traffic, and the Mafia can't push them out. They're split by jealousies and treacheries

[6]Andersen, "Crashing on Cocaine," *Time Magazine*, p. 29 (April 11, 1983).

[7]Phipp's, "FBI says bikers are 'public enemy No. 1,'" *Akron Beacon Journal*, (Sunday, December 6, 1981, p. B-1, col. 2).

[8]Williams and La Brecque, "And Now, the 'Israeli Mafia,'" *Newsweek*, p. 40 (January 5, 1981).

[9]"Yamaguchi-Gumi Mob Gets Rich at Funeral" (Associated Press, Thursday, October 26, 1981, p. 11-A, col. 1).

[10]News Article Short, *The Plain Dealer* (Wednesday, February 25, 1981, p. 4-F).

... It's just not the same organization that it was."[11]

The Mafia's problems have also created new twists on all old methods of problem solving. Due to the newer generation's unwillingness to soil their hands, or as some put it, their "weaknesses," as well as a lack of more embattled members, the Cosa Nostra has had to go to outsiders for certain services: drug transportation and distribution, numbers running, prostitution, and enforcement. Some of these outside contractual services have been forced upon the Mafia by circumstances, while others have arisen out of necessity. In some cases, for instance, the Mafia has had to import contract killers from Sicily to act as hit men because of the unavailability of some "local talent."[12] In addition, the Mafia has also contracted with outlaw motorcycle gangs, among others, for such services as murder, assault, loan shark collection, arson, and varied enforcement activities.[13] The shift from inside to outside for certain of these activities within some traditional organized crime groups will surely continue.

Aside from the shift from inside to outside the Mafia for the performance of certain essential, but soiled, services, another more subtle and somewhat more gradual transition of power is slowly taking place. In many parts of the country, the Mafia has used Blacks, Puerto Ricans, and Hispanics for many years as underlings and "go-fors" in its criminal enterprises, particularly in numbers operations, drug trafficking activities, and prostitution rings. As a consequence, these underlings have learned the business, its methods of operation, and its potentials for profit. A growing hunger for a piece of the action, as well as other factors, have contributed to the transition of some of these operations from Mafia controlled to minority controlled. Moreover, the increased minority awareness of the 1960s and the 1970s, particularly among Blacks, has also contributed to a growing trend toward

---

[11]Volkman, "Mother Mercy! Is This The End of La Cosa Nostra?" *Family Weekly*, p. 8 (February 13, 1983).

[12]Waller, "Generation Gap Forces Mafia to Support Killers From Sicily," *Canton Repository*, (NEA, Thursday, September 7, 1972, p. 34, col. 1).

[13]"Outlaw Motorcycle Gangs Turn to Organized Crime," *The Plain Dealer* (Associated Press, Wednesday, February 16, 1983, p. 17-A, col. 1).

takeover of certain rackets by former Mafia employed underlings, as well as other up-and-coming minority gangsters. This has been especially true as to rackets operated within the inner cities. The feeling seems to be that outsiders, i.e., white Mafioso, should not prey upon the slum minorities and that if a profit from such activities must be made it should be kept at home.

The takeover of illicit businesses heretofore operated by La Cosa Nostra is accomplished in several ways: sometimes force is used; often, minorities move in to fill voids created by the exit of other mobsters from the inner cities; on occasion, rackets owned by the Mafia are leased on a concession basis to minorities.[14] In some metropolitan areas, the transition is already complete, especially as to certain activities such as pimping and prostitution.[15]

Predictions for further ethnic progression or succession within organized crime have been made:

1. Gradual relinquishment of Italian/Sicilian-American control of organized crime and increased dominance by Blacks, Hispanics, Puerto Ricans, Chicanos, Cuban Americans, Colombians, and other minorities.[16]
2. Within some new groups, particularly as to the Blacks, loyalty will stem from relationships developed in early youth gangs and solidified in prison sects, unlike the Mafia kinship developed from familial ties.[17]
3. Black groups will emerge to dominate certain organized crime activities such as gambling and numbers operations, particularly within the inner cities, as well as prostitution.[18]
4. Chinese, Puerto Rican, Hispanic, and to a lesser extent, Black groups will control the heroin distribution network within the United States.[19]
5. Cuban and Colombian groups and perhaps the Israeli Mafia

---

[14]F. Ianni, *supra*, note 3, at 2.

[15]"Kings of Crime—Mafia Passes From Italian Families to Black Gangs, Expert Finds," *The Plain Dealer*, (New York Times Service, Monday, June 3, 1974, p. 8-A, col. 1).

[16]*Id.*

[17]F. Ianni, *supra*, note 3 at 10.

[18]*Kings of Crime, supra*, note 15.

[19]*Id.*

as well as other lesser-known gangs will continue to dominate the importation and distribution of most of the cocaine
and marijuana traffic within the United States.[20]

6. As with past powerful organized crime groups, Mafia interest will increasingly turn to legitimate business activities,
even if strong-arm and related illicit business methods continue to be used.

The process of ethnic succession and transition to power of new
groups will undoubtedly continue in the years ahead. The resulting
conflicts are likely to be bloody and disarming to all of society.

Aside from the transitional problems facing more established
and traditional segments of organized crime, business for all organized crime groups has continued to evolve into new areas, and in
some respects, the progression is out of and away from the old
(particularly with La Cosa Nostra). Organized crime has always
been astute in recognizing unfulfilled, unlawful consumer needs
or desires, targeting those who have the need or desire, its customers,
and then fulfilling those desires or needs to its own profit. Organized crime has also been especially adept at using existing
businesses and contacts to reach additional markets and consumers
to further its own profits. Thus, for example, organized crime is
continuing and will continue for some time to come with its
infiltration of legitimate business enterprises. This is accomplished
in many ways, some of which we have discussed in Chapter 4.
Continued investments and involvement can be expected in the
following areas:

1. Infiltration of legitimate business, including use of loansharking and gambling operations to gain footholds in such
businesses for manipulation by organized crime groups.
2. Planned bankruptcies as a result of its infiltration of some
legitimate businesses.
3. Planned thefts, burglaries, arsons, and insurance frauds as a
result of its infiltration of legitimate businesses.
4. Pornography, child pornography, pornography murders

---

[20]*Kings of Crime, supra*, note 15; *see also* Anderson, *supra*, note 6; Williams et al., *supra*,
note 8.

and rapes, abductions, and international forced prostitution.
5. Drugs.
6. Labor racketeering.
7. Contract scams.
8. Gambling, especially sports betting.
9. Use of illegal aliens in legitimate business enterprises.
10. Illegal dumping and disposal of toxic wastes, investments in coal, oil, and other energy ventures and unlawful manipulation of those ventures.
11. Record, video-tape, film, and tape piracy.
12. Health, dental, and medical care insurance frauds.
13. Fraudulent businesses, franchises, commodities, and the like.
14. Computer-assisted thefts.
15. ???

Several of these areas deserve and require special mention.

Organized crime's continuing takeover and infiltration of legitimate businesses, and its use of those businesses for a variety of unlawful purposes is a real threat; however, its threat to our economic system could have very far-reaching consequences. The trend will cause the quality of goods and services to deteriorate while prices will increase; legitimate competitors will be driven out of business or seriously harmed; taxes will be avoided; health and safety laws and regulations will be ignored, and the well-being of all of society will be adversely affected.

Organized crime's continuing involvement in pornography and prostitution will continue to have several rather heinous consequences to society. The easing of most social mores in this country over the last twenty years has, in part, increased the demand for more and more deviant sex act prostitution as well as similar pornographic material. As a consequence, organized crime has stepped in and provided for more deviant tastes. Child prostitutes are frequently available,[21] while child-child or child-adult pornographic films, pictures, and magazines are printed and distributed across the nation. Sex-act murders on film are available in some

---

[21]Hillibish, "Tale of Child Sex Exploitation Chilling," *The Repository* (Sunday, March 27, 1983, p. 8, col. 1).

areas of the country. Internationally, demand for caucasian prostitutes, particularly in Japan, has increased to the point where Yakuza crime groups (Japanese Mafia) have formed white slavery rings to lure unsuspecting, young, blond, caucasian females to Japan. Often, using talent agent fronts, the girls are provided with one-way tickets to Japan for promised legitimate entertainment employment, but upon arrival are forced or coerced into live performances demonstrating sex acts or prostitution activities.[22]

Organized crime's involvement in energy resources, one of the most critical modern-day problems facing this nation and the rest of the world, is extremely troublesome. Fraudulent business dealings, scams involving oil, gas, and coal leases, fencing of stolen mining and drilling equipment, and similar obvious activities are transpiring each day. However, the greatest threat lies in organized crimes' investment in such resources and its future manipulation of those resources for its own purposes.

The continuing importation and use of illegal aliens by both legitimate businesses and mob controlled legitimate businesses should be alarming to all. In bad economic times, the demands for these low-cost workers are perhaps higher than ever before. Competition in the marketplace and greed will surely solidify the continued use of such workers. American labor will continue to suffer in the process.

Organized crimes' involvement in toxic waste disposal is particularly alarming in light of the serious and long-standing potential health hazards associated with such waste. "Midnight dumping" is a booming industry[23] despite governmental efforts aimed at its control. Reportedly, such dumping has included sending toxic wastes to fictitious addresses C.O.D., burning contaminated oil wastes in apartment buildings to generate heat, and dumping chemicals on roadways or along roadways, in open fields, or even on city streets.[24] Mob ownership of dump sites where such wastes

---

[22]"Talent Agents Lure Star-Struck to Nightmare." *The Repository* (Associated Press, Sunday, April 11, 1982, p. 21, col. 1).

[23]Beck, Junkin, Taylor, Mandel, Agrest, and Achiron, "Storm Over the Environment," *Newsweek*, p. 16, 23 (March 7, 1983).

[24]*Id.*

have been unlawfully placed has already been well-documented.[25] Elimination of potential informers or witnesses has also occurred,[26] in light of recent federal probes into the problem.[27]

Although we can predict with some confidence, organized crimes' presence and probable involvement in these areas, one factor is quite clear: where profits can be made, with little risk, through the use of force, fear, intimidation, and if necessary corruption, organized crime will readily step in and fill any existing void. Continued investment by organized crime in these areas will be costly for all of society and dangerous as well. However, it will be undoubtedly profitable for organized crime.

[25]Anderson, "Mob Finds Hot New Racket: Toxic Wastes," *The Repository* (Sunday, November 16, 1980, p. 7, col. 1); Anderson, "Dump Site is Pegged to N.Y. Crime Family," *The Repository* (Tuesday, December 30, 1980, p. 7, col. 1).

[26]Beck, et al., *supra*, note 23.

[27]"Witness Charges Mob With Toxic Poisoning," *The Repository* (Associated Press, Wednesday, December 17, 1980, p. 13, col. 2).

Section II

Legal Issues in
Organized Crime Investigations

Chapter 6

ENFORCEMENT PROBLEMS

L aw enforcement traditionally has been faced with many severe, yet often seemingly simplistic, problems when confronting organized crime. Over the years, law enforcement has had great difficulty in not only identifying, isolating, and prosecuting organized crime principals but it has often had difficulty in even recognizing the existence of an organized crime problem per se.

Some years ago, for example, former United States Attorney General Ramsey Clark observed that, "Some Americans believe there is no such thing as organized crime. Others see organized crime as the scourge of the nation, the heart of the crime problem. One view is as far from the fact as the other. There is organized crime, and it is a serious problem."[1]

The President's 1967 Crime Commission conducted a survey of seventy-one cities to determine the extent of state and local efforts aimed at curbing organized crime. Of the seventy-one cities surveyed, only nineteen even admitted the presence of organized crime in their cities.[2] Astonishingly, forty-three police departments, including the Los Angeles, California, Police Department, answered that they had no organized crime in their area.[3]

These mistaken notions and unfounded opinions still permeate some areas of the nation and some law enforcement agencies as well. This refusal to admit the existence of organized crime is, in part, due to ignorance and fear; it is also due to information voids, improperly trained personnel, and corruption existing within particular agencies.

---

[1]R. Clark, Crime in America, p. 68 (Simon & Schuster, New York, New York 1970).

[2]President's Commission on Law Enforcement and Administration of Justice, The Challenge of Crime in a Free Society: A Report, p. 197 (Washington D.C., 1967).

[3]*Id.*

Regardless of the reasons for such misplaced and unsupportable beliefs, such beliefs have quite effectively hampered enforcement efforts. After all, it is really impossible to do anything about a problem if there is no recognition of the problem itself.

Gradually, as a result of Joseph Valachi's testimony and James Fratianno's revelations, numerous governmental hearings and findings, e.g., the President's 1967 Crime Commission *Report* and the 1976 Report of the Task Force on Organized Crime, most law enforcement agencies would today admit the existence of organized crime. In fact, most would hopefully agree with the 1976 Task Force on Organized Crime finding that "organized crime problems exist in every state and metropolitan area of the nation."[4]

Aside from these problems and those associated with the definitional considerations, which we discussed in Chapter 1, three main enforcement problems associated with organized crime investigations appear to be universal to all levels of enforcement.[5] These three problems as identified by the 1976 Task Force on Organized Crime are as follows:

1. There is a definite lack of research methodology associated with organized crime investigations and, therefore, a concomitant lack of systematic documentation as to its activities.
2. Law enforcement investigations are restricted by certain restraints that hamper control efforts directed at organized crime.
3. Law enforcement agencies fail to cooperate with other agencies' organized crime investigations, which ultimately hampers the overall enforcement effort.

In addition to these three critical problems, and those already discussed, law enforcement efforts to investigate and prosecute organized crime have been hampered by the following:

1. lack of funding;
2. lack of trained and motivated personnel;
3. lack of expertise sufficient to train personnel;

---

[4]National Advisory Committee on Criminal Justice Standards and Goals, Organized Crime: Report of the Task Force on Organized Crime, p. 2 (Washington D.C. 1976).

[5]*Id.* at 3.

4. lack of specialized enforcement and investigative units;
5. misplaced enforcement priorities; and
6. lack of enforcement tools sufficient to investigate and prosecute the problem.

In some instances, problems have been grossly magnified by the existence of one or more of these shortcomings. For example, in most enforcement units, budgetary decisions are based upon funding requests, which must include information about problem assessment, demonstrable needs, and hard empirical data. With the absence of problem recognition, awareness, assessment, and concomitant empirical data, funding in many instances cannot be obtained. The enforcement problem is thus magnified, and the problems build upon one another without interruption.

Traditional reactive law enforcement responses do not and cannot effectively deal with the problem of organized crime. Modern investigative methods must be employed if the problem is to be met even head-on. Although such responses have been strenuously criticized as aggressive law enforcement, subject to great potential for abuse and circumvention of personal liberties,[6] it must be clear that old enforcement notions and techniques simply do not work with organized crime.

In 1967, the President's Commission found that the traditional reactive law enforcement response was not sufficient in efforts directed against organized crime: "Prosecution based merely upon individual violations that come to the attention of law enforcement may result in someone's incarceration, but the criminal organization simply places someone else in the vacated position."[7]

Inasmuch as most organized crime activities are conducted clandestinely, standard or known research methods have simply not been effective in acquiring much useful information or evidence. Covert information collection methods are really of special significance in the investigation of organized crime. Such methods, principally electronic eavesdropping or wiretapping, as well as active, aggressive law enforcement infiltration of organized crime

---

[6]Applegate, "The Business Papers Rule: Personal Privacy and White Collar Crime," p. 16 *Akron Law Review*, 189, 206.

[7]*Report, supra,* note 2 at 199.

groups, often are severely criticized because of alleged violations and invasions of personal privacy. Although the use of such tools must be restricted to a degree to conform to constitutionally protected privacy areas (Fourth, Fifth, and Fourteenth Amendment considerations, see Chapter 9), many states have not even given state or local enforcement officers the right to pursue such information acquisition activities. As a consequence, enforcement efforts in such states are severely limited and often ineffectual.

The lack of effective legislation aimed at criminalizing participation in organized crime has also greatly hampered enforcement efforts. Although the federal government in its response to the problem of organized crime has provided some very effective statutes designed to constitutionally prohibit participation in criminal cartels (e.g., the RICO Statute, see Chapter 7), the states have been woefully slow in doing so. Moreover, the penalties that have been established as to some of the activities of organized crime (e.g., gambling, prostitution, etc.) have been little more than a slap on the wrist. Often, as quickly as individuals are arrested, they are back on the streets engaging in the very same enterprises that led to their original arrest. Even when they are detained for a time, or perhaps incarcerated as punishment for any offenses finally decided, someone else steps into the position from within the organization, which usually continues despite one or more individual prosecutions and/or incarcerations. As a partial consequence of this enforcement problem, officers have frequently been reluctant to spend a great deal of time on efforts that will have little real effect on an illegal and continuing operation. Thus, individual officer frustration in turn frustrates enforcement efforts on a much larger and ever-widening basis, when all such officers are considered in mass.

Until recently, for example, much emphasis was placed upon the use of only criminal sanctions to deal with the problems of organized crime. This further hampered efforts to curb or destroy organized crime groups because of the difficult criminal burdens that must be met in prosecutorial efforts conducted under and pursuant to criminal laws. Only in the last few years has any real effort been made to provide civil penalties for certain organized crime activities (see Chapter 7).

Perhaps the biggest, most frustrating enforcement problem of all has arisen because of the very nature of most organized criminal activity: The provision of desired but unlawful goods and services to a demanding public, which never seems to tire or thirst for such vices. Columnist Walter Lippmann seemed to have some insight into this enforcement problem when in 1931 he stated, "[Organized crime] . . . is the creature of our laws and conventions, and it is engulfed with our strongest appetites and our most cherished ideals. The fact that the underworld breaks the laws which we all respect in principle, that it employs methods, such as bribery, terrorism, and murder, which we all deeply deplore, should not divert our attention from the main point, which is that the underworld performs a function based ultimately upon a public demand."[8]

If any real progress is to be made from an enforcement standpoint, the findings of the President's 1967 Crime Commission *Report* and the 1976 *Task Force Report*, as well as the observations of Walter Lippmann and many others, must all be taken into account. An enforcement response if it is to be effective must include communitywide efforts involving police and other criminal justice agencies from both the federal and state governmental groups, the business community, and the public at large.

To be totally effective, the enforcement response must include the following essential elements:

1. Increased public awareness of all problems associated with organized criminal activity and all consequences flowing from that activity.
2. Development of adequate criminal and civil legislation aimed at punishing organized criminal activity and divesting that organization from its property and profits acquired in violation of criminal and civil laws.
3. Provision of adequate funding, properly trained personnel and enforcement tools, such as wiretapping legislation, to deal with the clandestine organized crime operations.

---

[8]Lippmann, W., "The Underworld: Our Silent Servant," *Forum, 85* (January): 1–4, 1931.

4. Cooperation between enforcement agencies at both the state and federal levels.

If these basic organized crime enforcement elements can be provided, consistent with a constitutionally protected system of government, enforcement efforts may yet stand a chance of success.

Chapter 7

THE FEDERAL RESPONSE

The federal response to organized crime since the turn of the century has been characterized by many as ineffective, even lethargic. Lethargic in its inability to check organized crime while often giving little more than lip service to much needed action. Attempts to combat organized crime through legislative action have always been reactive rather than prospective. As a result, organized crime has always been able to take the first step with the government following thereafter. Moreover, legislative action geared at addressing organized crime activity has often occurred only after intense public pressure. Little attention has been aimed at eliminating the causal factors providing the opportunity for organized crime to breed and grow. In-depth investigations into the causes and effects of organized crime that have been conducted over the years have often identified the variables that lead to organized criminal activities; sometimes, as a result of such inquiries, legislation has been passed providing some effective enforcement tools designed to combat organized crime.

The first in-depth federal investigation of crime in America was conducted from 1929 to 1932. Spawned by the increasing violence of the Twenties, President Herbert Hoover appointed George Woodward Wickersham, former Attorney General under President Taft, to chair the National Commission on Law Observance and Law Enforcement, which became popularly known as the Wickersham Commission. The three-year study undertaken by the Commission investigated all aspects of crime and law enforcement in the United States and presented its findings in a multivolume report. Some of the relevant findings of the Wickersham Commission concern the high cost of crime, particularly organized crime, both as to its illicit profits and the funding needed to combat it. Moreover, the Commission issued certain findings expressing the need for more information, research, and study of organized crime to allow for better understanding and the acquisition of greater knowledge as to organized crime's operations and structure in the hopes that appropriate measures might be taken to properly combat and prevent its growth. Events of time relegated this comprehensive report to a back shelf and little was done to implement any of its major recommendations.

Following World War II, several states began investigations into organized crime and following the release of the California and Chicago Crime Commission Reports an aspiring Senator from Tennessee set the mechanisms of the federal government in motion that were to bring organized crime into the national spotlight. On May 1, 1950, this Tennessee Senator, Estes Kevaufer, as Chairman of the United States Senate Special Committee to Investigate Organized Crime in Interstate Commerce, began hearings to ferret out facts about organized crime. In the following months, until its completion on September 1, 1951, the Committee provided organized crime with one of its most feared elements: notoriety. With hundreds of witnesses and hearings held in fourteen United States cities, often before national television audiences, the now famous Kefauver Committee studied organized crime.

Although often criticized as accomplishing no more than what was already known to many local public officials, of being a political catapult for its chairman, at time creating more myth than fact about organized crime and missing many of the most crucial leaders of the crime groups, the investigation cannot be considered a complete loss by any means. The investigation uncovered new information and lead to several positive actions. These were the Committee's major findings:

1. A national organized crime group called the Mafia was found to exist with operations in many major cities and was found to control gambling, prostitution, and many other vices.
2. Members of organized crime used interstate commerce to conduct and promote their illegal activities.
3. Gambling was a chief source of revenue for organized crime.
4. Organized crime was a local condition and that federal involvement was limited to (a) control of interstate aspects,

(b) indirect regulation, through a strengthening of tax laws, strengthening of fraud laws, and establishing more stringent record requirements, (c) more aggressive application of the laws to known or suspected gangsters, and (d) stricter immigration control.

Much was learned of the Mafia during these hearings, but too much emphasis was placed upon organized crime being synonymous with the term Mafia. For the next twenty years this concentration as we have seen continued to exist as to law enforcement efforts against organized crime groups.

In February of 1957, the Senate Committee on Government Operations formed a Senate Select Committee on Improper Activities in the Labor and Management Field to investigate illegal racketeering in union affairs. Under the guidance of Subcommittee Chairman Senator John L. McClellan, of Arkansas, and its Chief Counsel, Robert Kennedy, the investigation soon centered on one union in particular, the International Brotherhood of Teamsters, and on two individuals in control of that union: President Dave Beck and Central States Committee Leader James R. Hoffa, who was said to be second in command and heir apparent to Beck's office.

By the end of the Subcommittee hearings in 1960, evidence was uncovered that ultimately led to the incarceration of Beck and several other local union officials. Hoffa, however, was not convicted of any offense until 1962 (*Hoffa v. United States*, see Chapter 9). The investigations were instrumental in the structure and passage of the Labor/Management Reporting and Disclosure Act of 1959, as well as the Gambling Devices Act of 1962. In May of 1963, McClellan's Subcommittee became the Permanent Subcommittee on Investigations, which maintained its activity against organized crime.

McClellan's Subcommittee, with strong support from then Attorney General Robert Kennedy, was to provide a witness that would expose the Mafia or, as he called it, "La Cosa Nostra," to the country on national television. On September 27, 1963, an unknown sóldier, or soldati, or bottom-level member of the Genovese Family, took the stand and for the next five days told the inside story of the group referred to by outsiders as La Cosa Nostra or the Mafia. The testimony of this man, Joseph Valachi, provided the "biggest single intelligence breakthrough yet in combating organized crime and racketeering in the United States,"[1] at least according to Robert Kennedy. Valachi named names, places, dates, and events that coincided with information previously given the Justice Department by another exiled Mafioso, Nicola Gentile.

The McClellan Subcommittee certainly awakened the public to the workings of the Mafia and provided information that forced then FBI Director J. Edgar Hoover to recognize the existence of such an organization and move the FBI into active participation to combat the organization. Senator McClellan also introduced a bill that would have made it a crime to become a member of an organized crime group, particularly the Mafia, but the bill for certain constitutional reasons was never passed (see Chapters 1 and 9). The one and continuing major drawback to the McClellan Committee investigations centered on its continuing emphasis of the Mafia or La Cosa Nostra, thereby continuing the growing myth that the only organized crime group in the country was one of Italian/Sicilian origins. Such notions hampered more realistic approaches to the problem of organized crime and permitted many non-Italian/Sicilian groups to continue operations without much notoriety.

In addition to the investigations being conducted by members of Congress, the riots and civil disturbances of the mid 1960s, among other factors, led President Lyndon Baines Johnson to form the President's Commission on Law Enforcement and Administration of Justice to investigate all aspects of the United States criminal justice system. The Commission, which was composed of distinguished scholars and practitioners in the criminal justice field and related disciplines, conducted a thorough examination of crime in America. One segment of this massive investigation addressed organized crime and its impact upon the American public.

The Commission soon faced several major problems, most of which had also been faced by the Wickersham Committee. The

---

[1]P. Maas, *The Valachi Papers*, p. 9 (New York, G. P. Putnam & Sons, 1968).

Commission lacked the necessary tools to accomplish the goals they had endeavored to reach; normal research methodology would not lend itself to adaptation to the secretive and diverse nature of organized crime; information sources were restricted to previous research and investigative efforts; educated estimates were often limited to the minimal information available, and investigative efforts were greatly hampered by the lack of a standard definition for organized crime. Although some criticized the Commission's report as little more than compilations of already known information, the report provided much needed empirical data and correlated a multitude of previous information into a manageable form. In actuality, everyone concerned with this topic probably still benefits from the fine work and report issued by the President's 1967 Commission. Perhaps one of the greatest legacies of the Commission's report has been its exposure of the complexity of most organized crime groups and the difficulty in investigating and prosecuting those organized crime groups.

To overcome these problems and complexities, the Commission made certain recommendations, which included recommendations to strengthen existing legislation as well to enact new legislation. The end result of all the federal commission findings and investigations has concluded in the passage of an array of federal statutes applicable to any attack against organized crime when used in a cooperative approach by enforcement agencies. Through that legislation, enforcement agencies are equipped with certain tools to attack the structure, operations, and economic gains of organized crime in criminal and/or civil actions.

Of these statutes the following have been of some special significance to organized crime investigations.

1. *The Sherman Anti-Trust Act,* 15 U.S. Code §1 *et seq.* This Act basically prohibits agreements, conspiracies, or combinations in restraint of trade or commerce in interstate or foreign commerce. The Act provides both criminal as well as civil sanctions. Moreover, property obtained or held in violation of the Act may be forfeited upon application and hearing to the United States. The Act has proved useful in certain

monopolistic organized crime enterprises and has proved to
be a very useful federal tool.

2. *The Clayton Act,* contained in 15 U.S. Code §16 *et seq.* The
Clayton Act prohibits certain business practices that are aimed
at eliminating competition. The Act is really an outgrowth
of sorts of the Sherman Anti-Trust Act and, like that Act,
provides certain civil and criminal penalties.

3. *The Robinson-Patman Act,* 15 U.S. Code §13. This Act generally
prohibits discrimination as to prices for goods and services
and is aimed at prohibiting the use of unreasonably low prices
to destroy competition. The Act, which is a portion of the
Clayton Act, also provides certain criminal and civil penalties.

4. *The Hobbs Anti-Racketeering Act,* 18 U.S. Code §1951 *et seq.*
This Act is designed to criminalize certain activity, e.g. robbery or extortion, or attempts or conspiracies to do so, that
affect commerce or the movement of any article in commerce,
or that threatens violence to any person or property in
furtherance of some conspiracy to violate the Act. The Act
provides for imprisonment for a period not to exceed twenty
years and/or the imposition of a fine not to exceed $10,000
upon conviction. Other sections of Chapter 95 of the United
States Code, which followed the enactment of 18 U.S. Code
§1951, commonly known as the Hobbs Anti-Racketeering
Act, also specifically prohibit the travel in the interstate or
foreign commerce or the use of any facility of interstate or
foreign commerce, including the mail, to commit certain
specified criminal acts (see §18 U.S. Code §1952). Other
related sections of the Anti-Racketeering Statute, provide for
penalties for the interstate or foreign transportation of
wagering or gambling paraphernalia. §1955 of Title 18 of the
United States Code, also prohibited *inter alia*, the management or supervision of an illegal gambling business as defined by the statute. This section of Title 18 of the United
States Code, was passed as a portion of Public Law 91-452 in
1970. That Law also created The Commission on the Review
of the National Policy Towards Gambling, which ultimately
issued a comprehensive report, which has been quoted

throughout this work. Finally, §1954 of Title 18 sought to criminalize the offer, acceptance, or solicitation of a bribe to influence the operations of an employee benefit plan. Aside from the original provisions of the Hobbs Anti-Racketeering Act now contained in 18 United States Code §1951, which provided for a penalty of $10,000.00 and imprisonment for not more than twenty years, the other cited sections now contained in Chapter 95 of the United States Code, provide for penalties of imprisonment not more than three or five years and a fine not to exceed $10,000.

5. *The Omnibus Crime Control and Safe Streets Act of 1968.* The Omnibus Crime Control and Safe Streets Act of 1968 was passed as a direct result of the President's Commission on Law Enforcement and Administration of Justice. While many of the Acts' provisions dealt with the creation of LEAA and certain educational and research projects, the Law also contains sections on firearms and wiretapping. The most significant aspect of the law dealt with the creation of a framework within which law enforcement officers could seek and obtain authorization for conducting wiretaps and other electronic surveillance. These Sections, which were passed pursuant to Title III of the Act, are now contained in 18 United States Code §2510 *et seq.* (see Chapter 9).

6. *Organized Crime Control Act of 1970,* Public Law 91-452. The Organized Crime Control Act of 1970 created very specific provisions to deal with the problem of organized crime. Sections of the Act have been interspersed in Title 18 of United States Code. The Organized Crime Control Act is composed of thirteen separate Titles. Although we have discussed each of these Titles throughout the work, it is important to point out that the Organized Crime Control Act provided for grants of immunity as to certain witnesses, the establishment of protection facilities and housing for government witnesses, specific provisions as to interstate gambling, and most importantly, the establishment of the Racketeer Influenced and Corrupt Organizations Chapter, now codified in 18 U.S. Code Section 1961 *et seq.* The RICO

Statute has become the foremost tool in the federal government's efforts against organized crime at the national level. The Act itself is designed to punish participation in criminal syndicates by both civil and criminal penalties. Increasingly, the Act has become a most useful tool in the federal efforts against organized crime.

7. A series of other miscellaneous federal laws have been used to counteract the problems of organized crime. Certain of these have been passed within the Internal Revenue Code while others have been passed within the Food and Drug Code now contained in 21 U.S. Code §801 *et seq.* Several sentencing statutes have also been developed that provide for forfeitures of certain property used in the commission of certain specified crimes. These are contained in 18 U.S. Code §3611 *et seq.*

In efforts to deal with organized crime at the federal level, several unique concepts have developed, among which is the Strike Force approach to organized crime investigations. Under this approach, first developed by former Attorney General Ramsey Clark, members of various United States enforcement agencies are coordinated in teams under a specified United States Attorney to coordinate intense efforts directed against particularly targeted groups or individuals. Often, the strike force approach has been effective and continues to be utilized by more current Attorney Generals.

Other federal efforts directed at theft and fencing operations have also been very successful in recovering millions of dollars of merchandise and in at least temporarily stopping the free-flow of illicit goods through the underground economy. These federal efforts, commonly known as sting operations, have attempted to utilize undercover operations to recover stolen property and merchandise. Quite frequently, insurance companies agree to provide funds for these undercover fencing operations, while the fencing operations themselves are video-taped or filmed, and detailed records are kept of the various transactions. Following the sting operations, federal enforcement units through special or regular Grand Jury proceedings issue indictments and officers then proceed to round up those indicted persons dealing with the undercover sting fencing operation. Following the arrests, prosecutions utilizing the video tape and/or film record materials are begun. New coordinated efforts among the various federal enforcement agencies are presently underway, which should prove to be somewhat more effective than past efforts. The FBI has finally made a determination to enter the drug investigation and enforcement area together with the Drug Enforcement Administration (DEA) and together, particularly with the aid of sophisticated electronic and radar tracking equipment, they should prove to be most effective. Coordinated efforts between the Internal Revenue Service and other federal agencies such as the FBI, the DEA, the Alcohol, Tobacco and Firearms Department, together with miscellaneous enforcement agencies should prove to be most effective in continuing efforts against organized crime.

On occasion, federal government efforts have been directed toward foreign governments to assist in organized crime enforcement programs. Most particularly, efforts by the federal government over the last ten years in the area of drug control have solicited the cooperation of foreign governments, particularly those of Turkey and Mexico and other opium producing or marijuana producing countries, to assist in stopping the growth and/or processing of illicit drugs, particularly heroin.

Continued efforts at the federal government level should make significant progress toward the problems of organized crime. Anything less than total, aggressive utilization of federal enforcement tools will not, however, eradicate or even dent the problem of organized crime. The recent formation of a Presidential twenty-member commission on Organized Crime may assist in this effort inasmuch as its stated aim is "to break apart and cripple . . . organized crime syndicates. . . . "[2]

---

[2]"Crime Commission to Travel," *The Repository*, P. 3, col, 1, (Friday, July 29, 1983).

Chapter 8

THE STATE RESPONSE

Although there seems to be little question that organized crime is a national, even an international, problem, enforcement heretofore has fallen mainly upon the states' shoulders. This is true even though specific federal laws have been passed proscribing certain organized crime conduct and activities (see Chapter 7). Assuming enforcement is primarily a state matter, the states' responses have, for the most part, been woefully inadequate.

Perhaps one of the biggest problems in state efforts to develop effective enforcement as to organized crime has stemmed from many of the states' fragmented political systems. Often these systems have at their base city, township, burrough, or other local governmental entities, employing prosecutors (municipal prosecutors) and maintaining police agencies (city, village, or township police forces). Geographically larger governmental units such as counties also typically have prosecuting attorneys (county prosecutors) and police enforcement units (sheriff's departments). Most states also have a third and final tier including a state prosecutor (attorney general) and a state police agency (state police). Within this three-tiered structure exists a host of specialized enforcement units with varying law enforcement powers, such as state liquor, tax, arson, securities, and business investigative units. These units primarily derive their power from state administrative agencies created and empowered by state statute.

This rather loose, fragmented, and diverse enforcement system is cherished by many. However, in many respects it has greatly inhibited investigations as well as prosecutions of organized crime members. Political jealousies existing among the various tiers or even within the same tiers and between different departments or agencies has further hampered cooperation in investigations and prosecutions of organized crime figures. Consequently, some of these departments have not benefited in many instances from the investigative efforts and accumulated knowledge of other departments. Since organized crime does not limit its activities to artificial political boundaries, one can readily see the enforcement problems that can arise as a result of such fragmented, disjointed responses by a host of agencies lacking essential facts and information often possessed by other agencies.

In many states, jurisdictional jealousies have developed between such groups as county prosecuting attorneys and state attorney general's office. Typically, state attorney general's offices have sought more centralized investigative and enforcement powers as to organized crime investigations, while local prosecutors have done their best to retain such investigative and prosecutorial power at their level. The problem has limited cooperation between such groups, and again it has hampered coordinated organized crime investigation and enforcement efforts. The respective national associations for each group (Attorney Generals: The National Association of Attorneys General; Prosecutors: The National District Attorneys Association) have each supported their individual member's positions to varying degrees and sought to maintain or gain more powers in this area for its members. The problems have thus become magnified.

In some instances, efforts have been put forth as compromise measures to grant more centralized power to state agencies or attorney general's offices so that more effective enforcement might take place. Ohio promulgated such a compromise measure in 1970 that granted certain specified powers to the state attorney general's office. The statute however, granted little real power to the Ohio Attorney General. Such legislative efforts it would seem are more effective at compromising political and jurisdictional jealousies than in dealing with the problems of organized crime. Ohio's response as to the grant of limited powers due to political infighting among enforcement groups is typical of many states' responses in this area.

Aside from the lack of cooperation within state and local governmental enforcement agencies, there have been more problems in even attempting coordination of enforcement or cooperation between federal agencies and state and local units. The internal state problem is therefore also a national problem, and in many areas joint efforts between federal and state or local agencies to enforce laws against organized crime are nonexistent. In large part this lack of cooperation is again due to petty political and jurisdictional jealousies. In certain cases, however, it is also due to past efforts at cooperation, some of which resulted in leaks of information, thereby exposing corruption and graft. Such instances certainly do not lead to trust between enforcement units and have contributed to the cooperation and coordination problems.

The political and jurisdictional jealousies between agencies have adversely affected the state's enforcement response to organized crime in the following material respects:

1. *Lack of enforcement coordination.* Since organized crime does not limit itself to particular jurisdictions, any lack of enforcement coordination of a multijurisdictional criminal operation ultimately hampers or dooms the enforcement effort.
2. *Lack of enforcement cooperation.* Without cooperation between jurisdictions where organized crime operates, agencies incur additional and duplicate costs, efforts to acquire information overlap, and the chances for exposure and leaks of information greatly increase.
3. *Lack of enforcement information exchange.* If agencies do not share acquired information regarding organized crime, a total and sophisticated analysis of that information is all but impossible, the big picture is consequently often overlooked while strategic planning suffers.
4. *Lack of overall enforcement strategy.* Agencies that do not cooperate or exchange information cannot possibly develop an effective strategy or plan to combat the organized crime problem.
5. *Lack of enforcement power.* Although primarily a jurisdictional problem rather than an enforcement problem arising as a result of jurisdictional jealousies, inability of any government enforcement officer to cross jurisdictional lines greatly diminishes any single unit's ability to even investigate organized crime no less develop any case against its members.

Jurisdictional and political problems as well as the lack of agency cooperation and coordination are only a few of the problems that have adversely affected the state's response to the problem of organized crime. For many years some states and major metropolitan areas have failed to recognize that they even had an organized crime problem. During the 1965 to 1967 investigation by the President's Crime Commission for example, only nineteen cities out of seventy-one surveyed by the Commission acknowledged having organized crime within their jurisdictions.[1] Obviously, investigation and correction of any problem is nearly impossible if there is no recognition of the problem.

State enforcement of the problem of organized crime has also been greatly hampered by a lack of sufficient funds as well as the lack of public awareness about the problems associated with this type of criminal activity. Funding for any enforcement response to organized crime has always been somewhat sparse, in large part due to legislators' unwillingness to recognize either the threat of organized crime or the magnitude of the problem. Moreover funding of organized crime enforcement programs has for the most part, been a *reaction* to a particular event, e.g., notorious gangland slayings, rather than a well-reasoned, planned strategy to deal with the problem in advance of some action-spurring event. Funding has thus been reactive and sporadic rather than planned.

Public pressure for either funding or action has never been fully realized, largely because of a lack of problem awareness and information, a lack of interest and to some degree an unwillingness to demand action against a group supplying desired goods and services, e.g., gambling, loansharking, drugs, and prostitution. Many people do not perceive the organized crime problem as a problem because many willingly participate in its marketplace activities; after all, what harm can come from a sports bet with the local bookie or a purchase of a small bag of marijuana from the local dealer. Such complacent attitudes are still present in many communities.

State lawmakers have also hampered law enforcement efforts to deal with organized crime by often failing to provide them with necessary information tools. For example, in 1967 a majority of

---

[1]President's Commission on Law Enforcement and Administration of Justice, *The Challenge of Crime in a Free Society: A Report*, p. 197 (Washington D.C. 1967).

the President's Crime Commission recognized the need for the enactment of legislation allowing electronic surveillance in organized crime investigations. Some authorities, moreover, have concluded that electronic surveillance is "the single most valuable weapon in law enforcement's fight against organized crime."[2] The Special Committee on Standards for the Administration of Criminal Justice of the American Bar Association concluded after exhaustive study and discussion as to electronic surveillance in its 1971 *Standards Related to Electronic Surveillance* that, "We [the Committee and ultimately the ABA when the Standards were approved in 1971 by the ABA House of Delegates] believe . . . that there is a compelling social need to enforce the penal law in the area of organized crime. . . . We therefore, find that the use of electronic surveillance techniques is necessary in the administration of justice in the area of organized crime."[3]

The Task Force Report on Organized Crime stated in its 1976 *Report:*

> Because of their organization and methods of operation, organized crime activities require sophisticated means of evidence gathering. Often witnesses will not come forward; and members of some organizations are bound either by an oath of silence or threats of violence. Often the use of informants is of limited value, and many organizations are difficult, if not impossible, for undercover agents to penetrate to the point where they can obtain useful evidence.
>
> One way to break through these conspiratorial safeguards is to enact a State Statute permitting nonconsensual wiretap and microphonic surveillance. States should recognize the conflicting needs of effective law enforcement and individual rights and provide for adequate protection of such rights by statute consistent with the problem of organized crime within their own jurisdictions.[4]

The need for such authorizing and enabling legislation can hardly be questioned in light of these findings and recommendations. However, less than half the states allow such electronic sur-

---

[2]*Id.* at p. 201 (quote attributed to New York County District Attorney Frank S. Hogan).

[3]American Bar Association, *Standards Relating to Electronic Surveillance*, p. 96 (Approved Draft 1971).

[4]National Advisory Committee on Criminal Justice Standards and Goals, Report of the Task Force on Organized Crime, p. 148 (Washington D.C. 1976).

veillance. Some states specifically prohibit it and in fact make a non-consenual interception of telephone communications a criminal act.

Various state crime commissions or councils formed to study state problems caused by organized crime have repeatedly concluded that there is an absolute need for such a tool and recommended state passage of such legislation. These recommendations, for example, have been made in Illinois, Massachusetts, New York, Ohio, and Pennsylvania, among many other states. Yet, the need has gone unmet in many jurisdictions, even those whose commissions have found the existence of significant organized crime problems in their own states, e.g., Ohio.

Strenuous arguments have been put forth by several segments of society in opposition to the enactment of electronic surveillance statutes. The American Civil Liberties Union, among others, has been in the forefront of opposition to the further enactment of legislation authorizing electronic surveillance.[5]

There is little question, however, that legislation can be constitutionally enacted (see Chapter 9). In 1968, Title III of the Omnibus Crime Control and Safe Streets Act was passed into law by Congress.[6] The Act, although prohibiting the electronic interception of wire or oral communications, excepted from the law those interceptions by law enforcement officers authorized by a court pursuant to an investigation of certain specified crimes, which for the most part constitute serious felonies. Moreover, as we shall examine in Chapter 9, properly drawn legislation is not in contravention of the United States Constitution nor United States Supreme Court cases construing that charter. Arguments such as those advanced in Ohio against the passage of such legislation are often more founded in emotion than fact.[7]

---

[5]"Rhodes Aims Two Bills at Organized Crime", *The Plain Dealer*, p. 10D, Sept. 11, 1981.

[6]See 18 U.S.C. §§2510–2520 (1968).

[7]Although there may be abuses from time to time (see Berreby, "5 Lawyers Bugged by F.B.I.; Class Action Suit Planned," *The National Law Journal*, p. 2, Mon. July 13, 1981), such instances are rare especially as to conversations protected by the Constitution or other law (privileged communications and the like).

State prosecution of organized crime figures has also been hampered by a lack of "serious crime" legislation for some criminal acts. For example, many states proscribe gambling activities as well as prostitution but designate the crimes as misdemeanors. Others designate promotion of gambling, promotion of prostitution, sports betting, some drug offenses, thefts, and frauds as lower degree felonies, most of which are probationable. In such states it is very difficult, if not impossible, to elevate any ongoing criminal conspiracy such as organized crime into a more serious felony. As a consequence, individuals participating in such conspiracies are often treated as minor offenders. Management and participation in such conspiracies therefore continues without much interruption as a result of conviction for a serious felony.

Some states have sought to enact legislation similar to the federal R.I.C.O. law (see Chapter 7) to increase the seriousness and concomitant penalties for the commission of organized criminal activity. Some of these statutes, as we shall discuss in Chapter 9, have run into conflict with constitutional requirements. While others have not, there seems to be a clear law enforcement need for such legislation if organized crime operations are to be appropriately punished. Ohio's 1982 Organized Crime Report seems to most adequately state the need: "Without a State Racketeering Statute in Ohio, . . . law enforcement will likely fail to put organized crime out of business. Without [this statute] . . . law enforcement in Ohio will never have the tools to attack the organization, the enterprise or the pattern of criminal activity which is at the core of the effort of organized crime to acquire power and profit.[8]

Although problems abound, state responses to organized crime have taken shape at least to a degree. In 1967, the President's Crime Commission recommended the following for state action:

1. Establishment of citizen and business organization crime commissions.
2. Establishment of state organized crime investigative com-

---

[8]Law Enforcement Consulting Committee, Report to the Governor of Ohio on Organized Crime, pp. 155–6 (State of Ohio, Columbus, Ohio 1982).

missions, with independent, permanent staffs and subpoena powers.

3. Private business association development of strategies to uncover and prevent organized crime infiltration into legitimate businesses.
4. Increased dissemenation of information about organized crime by government and private sector groups.
5. Creation of specialized investigative and prosecutorial units in state attorney general's offices, prosecutor's offices, and police departments.
6. Encouragement of greater interdepartment and interagency cooperation and exchange of information about organized crime.
7. Enactment of legislation to provide extended prison terms for managerial or supervisory organized crime personnel.
8. Creation of special grand juries to investigate and, if appropriate, indict organized crime personnel.
9. Enactment of new witness immunity laws to encourage broader testimony of insiders in organized crime cases.
10. Establishment of certain procedural changes in evidentiary rules for prosecution of organized crime individuals and activities.

Some states have taken up these recommendations. State organized crime commissions have been created, for example, in New York, New Jersey, Pennsylvania, New Mexico, and Hawaii whose primary missions are investigation and dissemination of information about organized crime to law enforcement agencies as well as the public. Other states, such as Ohio, have created organized crime commissions but with less powers, e.g., no subpoena power, limited funding, limited access to information, and limited staffs. As a consequence, the full potential of these commissions probably will never be realized.

Other states have enacted legislation designed to increase the penalties for organized criminal activities. Some states have centralized investigations to a degree as to organized crime figures, increased the exchange of information about those activities, and even cooperated in building cases for prosecution. In California, for example, a Law Enforcement Intelligence Network was established to facilitate the exchange of information about organized crime. In addition, regional enforcement networks have also been established in most areas of the country to further encourage the greater exchange of organized crime intelligence. Special grand juries have been used in various locals and some modifications of evidence rules have taken place in some states so as to assist in the successful prosecution of organized crime figures.

It yet remains to be seen if these beginnings will serve as solid foundations for better, more successful investigations and prosecutions of organized crime members. It also remains to be seen if the state's response can assist in curbing the tide of organized crime.

Section III

Investigations of Organized Crime

Chapter 9

SELECTED CONSTITUTIONAL AND LEGAL ISSUES IN INVESTIGATIONS AND PROSECUTIONS

Investigations and prosecutions of organized crime figures are subject to certain constitutional guarantees and legal restraints. Issues regarding individual rights, privacy, search and seizure, arrest and detention, interrogation and confession, equal protection, immunity, and general due process are all potential subjects to any comprehensive discussion of organized crime enforcement. The Constitution, as the highest source of United States law, must serve as a starting point for these discussions.

As in all criminal matters, certain constitutional safeguards protect the rights of those accused of criminal conduct including those associated with organized crime. Of particular importance to organized crime investigations are the Fourth, Fifth, Fourteenth, and to a lesser degree, the Sixth Amendment to the United States Constitution. A brief review of the Amendments and certain significant cases interpreting these Amendments, with concentration upon their application to organized crime investigations, would seem to be in order.

The Fourth Amendment to the United States Constitution provides:

> The right of the people to be secure in their persons, houses, papers, and effects, against unreasonable searches and seizures, shall not be violated, and no warrants shall issue, but upon probable cause, supported by oath or affirmation, and particularly describing the place to be searched, and the persons or things to be seized.

These protections afforded by the United States Constitution are for the most part mirrored, as with all the Amendments, by similar state constitutional protections. The Fourth Amendment is basically a restraint upon the federal government and its agents. It prevents unreasonable intrusions into a person's home or as to his papers and effects. It, however, protects persons as well as property from unwarranted governmental intrusion (*Katz v United States*, 389 US 347, 1967).

Generally, searches without a warrant are unlawful and unreasonable, unless the search falls within certain defined exceptions (see *United States v Ventresca*, 380 US 102, 1965). These exceptions might be broken down by category as follows:

1. *Searches Incident to a Lawful Arrest.* A law enforcement officer may conduct a full custodial search of a subject's person and the area within his immediate reach contemporaneously with a lawful arrest (*United States v Robinson*, 414 US 218, 1973; *Gustafson v Florida*, 414 US 260, 1973; *Chimel v California*, 395 US 1752, 1969; see also *United States v Edwards*, 415 US 800, 1974).

2. *Searches Pursuant to a Valid Consent.* A law enforcement officer may conduct a search pursuant to a valid consent, provided that a finding is made that the consenting person had the right to consent and gave that consent freely, voluntarily, and knowingly, so as to constitute a waiver of a known constitutional right (see, e.g., *Bumper v North Carolina*, 391 US 543, 1968).

3. *Searches Under Stop and Frisk Circumstances.* Under the doctrine first laid down in *Terry v Ohio*, 392 US 1 (1968), a law enforcement officer may conduct a limited "pat down" of a suspect's outer clothing where he has reasonable suspicion to believe that criminal activity is taking place and that a pat down is necessary to protect the safety of persons in the area or himself.

4. *Seizure of Objects in Plain View.* An item that is in open, plain view that is evidence of a crime may be seized by a law enforcement officer (*Harris v United States*, 390 US 234, 1967) if the law enforcement officer is in a place where he has a right to be (*Warden v Hayden*, 387 US 294, 1967; see also *Texas v Brown*, 81–419, 1983).

5. *Searches Under Emergency Circumstances.* Under certain emer-

gency conditions, officers may enter premises to affect an arrest (*Warden v. Hayden*, 387 US 294, 1967).

6. *Searches of Vehicles.* Searches of vehicles, if stopped while in transit or while same were capable of movement, have been upheld in certain cases if there was probable cause and insufficient time to get a warrant (*Brinegar v. United States*, 338 US 160, 1949; see also *Chambers v. Maroney*, 399 US 42, 1970). Such a search however must occur within a reasonable time (*Collidge v. New Hampshire*, 403 US 443, 1971).

In the absence of one of these exceptions, a search will generally be condemned unless a warrant was obtained beforehand authorizing the intrusion. If no warrant in such a circumstance is obtained, the evidence obtained from the search will be supressed and excluded from court consideration (*Weeks v. United States*, 232 US 382, 1914). The *Weeks* holding applied to federal law enforcement officers, although it was made binding upon the states in *Mapp v. Ohio*, 367 US 643 (1961). The "Exclusionary Rule" as developed by *Weeks* and *Mapp* applied to evidence seized in violation of Constitutional requirements as well as any evidence derived from that illegally obtained evidence, i.e., the fruits of such a search (*Wong Sun v. United States*, 371 US 471, 1963) establishing the so-called "fruits of the poisonous tree doctrine."

The exclusionary rule as developed by *Weeks* and *Mapp* has been very severely criticized (see Chief Justice Berger's dissent in *Bivens v. Six Unknown Named Agents of the Federal Bureau of Narcotics*, 403 US 388, 1971). The rule, originally designed to prevent technically unlawful police conduct, in light of citizen respect for the law, has been criticized because it really perverts the true finding process of the jury by removing otherwise relevant and important evidence from their consideration (see Herbert, "ABA's Response to Proposals to Modify the Exclusionary Rule," *Judges Journal*, 1975).

The Supreme Court has refused to extend the exclusionary rule to grand jury deliberations (*United States v. Calandra*, 414 US 338, 1974). Similarly, the Court has also refused to extend the rule to federal civil proceedings (*United States v. Janis*, 428 US 433, 1976). In such situations, therefore, evidence, even if obtained in violation of the Fourth Amendment constitutional requirements, reaches and is considered by the fact finders at such proceedings. At present, a case is pending before the United States Supreme Court to determine whether or not the rule will be abolished (see *Illinois u Gates*, #81-430). Regardless of the outcome of that case, it is clear that the rule will continue to be eroded, perhaps to the point of extinction.

Particular Fourth Amendment issues are singularly important to any study of organized crime. This is largely due to the nature of organized criminal activity and its methods of operation. The President's Crime Commission in 1967 made the following findings:

> [C]ommunication is essential to the operation of any business enterprise. In legitimate business this is accomplished with written and oral exchanges. In organized crime enterprises, however, the possibility of loss or seizure of an incriminating document demands a minimum of written communication. Because of the varied character of organized criminal enterprises, the large numbers of persons employed in them, and frequently the distances separating elements of the organization, the telephone remains an essential vehicle for communication. While discussions of business matters are held on a face-to-face basis whenever possible, they are never conducted in the presence of strangers. Thus, the content of these conversations, including the planning of new illegal activity, and transmission of policy decisions or operating instructions for existing enterprises, cannot be detected.[1]

Often, the transmittal of communicative messages between organized crime individuals requires those individuals to take extreme steps to avoid observation and detection of the message. Frequently, they will move from place to place to ensure that they are not followed prior to having a face-to-face meeting with another member for various criminal purposes. As a consequence, law enforcement has responded in some respects in an effort to track those movements with certain electronic aids. One of these tracking devices, commonly known as a "beeper," has been used by law enforcement quite extensively to follow organized crime members as well as others. The beepers are generally attached to an automobile or moveable piece of personal property, e.g., a suitcase, and

---

[1]The President's Commission on Law Enforcement and Administration of Justice, *The Challenge of Crime in a Free Society: A Report*, p. 201 (Washington D.C., 1967).

through an electronic emission from the beeper the subjects are followed or tracked by agents with an electronic receiver. In this manner, an individual can be traced even if he or she is not within eyesight. Particular constitutional questions have arisen in such situations that have only recently been decided by the U.S. Supreme Court in *United States v. Knotts*, 103 S. Ct. 1081 (1983). Two principal issues involve the use of these tracking devices. The first involves the question of whether or not the *warrantless installation* of such devices is a violation of the Fourth Amendment protections, while the second involves the question of whether or not the cumulative tracking process invades an individual's reasonable expectations of privacy. While the Supreme Court has yet to decide the first of these issues, it has held in the *Knotts* case that the tracking of individuals over public highways and into private areas is not a search and not a seizure. The resolution of the first issue will generally depend upon the conditions of the warrantless installations and the nature of the interests invaded by law enforcement agents (see, e.g., *Miroyan v. United States/McGinnis v. United States*, 439 U.S. 1338 1978; *United States v. Michael*, 645 F. 2d 252, 5th Cir. 1980).

While the *Knotts* decision ultimately turned upon the issue of reasonable expectation of privacy, the beeper cases also deal with the tracking of movement; nothing is actually seized other than the knowledge of movement and the location. No property is taken, and no conversation is overheard or seized. There may be a brief trespass in particular cases for attachment of the beeper, even a somewhat lengthy trespass if the presence of the beeper is also viewed as a continuing trespass; however, there is no actual physical intrusion inside a car, plane, house, or phone booth.

Constitutional safeguards have become more stringent when the activity under scrutiny is clearly a search and/or a seizure, when there is a taking, and when there is a trespass and an actual physical intrusion. In such cases, zones of privacy and reasonable expectations of privacy are clearly entered and perhaps violated.

In organized crime investigations, efforts to acquire or learn information have often been greatly hampered. The 1976 Task Force Report on Organized Crime stated:

Because of their organization and methods of operation, organized crime activities require sophisticated means of evidence gathering. Often witnesses will not come forward; and members of some organizations are bound either by an oath of silence or threats of violence. Often the use of information is of limited value, and many organizations are difficult, if not impossible, for undercover agents to penetrate to the point where they can obtain useful evidence.

One way to break through these conspiratorial safeguards is to enact a State Statute permitting non-consensual wiretaps and microphonic surveillance. States should recognize the conflicting needs of effective law enforcement and individual rights and provide for adequate protection of such rights by statute consistent with the problem of organized crime within their own jurisdiction.[2]

In order to pierce such organizations, law enforcement began to turn to electronic eavesdropping of oral communications and wiretapping of telephone conversations of organized crime members. Their efforts lead to the development of a significant body of constitutional and statutory law. The development of this law really began with *Olmstead v United States*, 277 U.S. 438(1928). In this case, agents "tapped" telephone lines of one Olmstead who was a principal in a large-scale conspiracy to violate the National Prohibition Act. The tapping was accomplished without actual trespass upon private property. Incriminating statements were overheard during the taps and used against the defendants at trial.

The defense asserted that their Fourth Amendment and Fifth Amendment rights were violated. The Court, after examining and stating the issues, held that absent actual physical trespass there could be no entry into a protected zone so as to raise Fourth Amendment issues. Moreover, the Court concluded that the Fifth Amendment question was inapplicable absent compelled conversation; since the defendants were not forced to provide incriminating statements but rather provided such statements over the telephone freely and voluntarily, the Fifth Amendment prohibitions were inapplicable.

Following the *Olmstead* decision, a second significant case arose before the Supreme Court in 1942. This case, *Goldman v United States*, 316 U.S. 129, questioned law enforcement agents' utilization

---

[2]*The Task Force on Organized Crime*, p. 148 (1976).

of a "detectaphone," or listening device, to overhear certain incriminating statements made by the defendants within the office of one of the principals. The detectaphone was placed against a common wall within that office in a room legitimately occupied by the agents; the wall was not penetrated by the agents, but even so, the statements were obtained, transcribed, and ultimately used at trial against the defendants. The Supreme Court again held that absent an actual physical trespass *into* a protected area, no Fourth Amendment violation can occur.

Some years later, in *Silverman v United States*, 365 U.S. 505 (1961), the Court again considered a new twist to the facts as decided in the *Olmstead* and *Goldman* case. In *Silverman*, law enforcement officers used a microphone spike listening device, inserted into and through a common wall of a defendants' row house where suspected gambling activities were taking place. Although the spike did not pierce the actual interior walls of the defendants' house, it did abut up against that wall and used a portion of that abutment as a sounding board to pick up incriminating conversation later used at trial. The Court in examining the facts and comparing them principally to the *Goldman* case reasoned that the employment of the spike amounted to a trespass of a "constitutionally protected area."

The controversy surrounding the employment of electronic or mechanical devices to surreptitiously pick up incriminating statements was finally resolved by the Supreme Court in *Katz v United States*, 389 U.S. 347 (1967). In *Katz* the Court considered whether the employment of a listening device on the outside of a telephone booth wall to record incriminating conversations amounted to an impermissible intrusion into a constitutionally protected area. The Court answered this question in the affirmative and held that *any* intrusion (even without accompanying physical trespass) into a constitutionally protected area must be declared violative of the Fourth Amendment. In holding that the Fourth Amendment protects "people and not simply 'areas' against unreasonable searches and seizures" the Court effectively required the issuance of judicially granted warrants for such intrusions.

After *Katz* there was no longer much room for argument that unauthorized electronic bugging or wiretapping was not prohibited by the Fourth Amendment. In fact, *Katz* made clear the need for judicial and warrant protections before such intrusions were constitutionally permissible. As a partial consequence of *Katz*, and as a part of the comprehensive legislation following the President's 1967 Crime Report, Congress on June 19, 1968, passed the Omnibus Crime Control and Safe Streets Act of 1968. As a portion of that Act, Congress enacted a Wiretapping and Electronic Surveillance Statute, which is contained in 18 USC Section 2510 *et seq.* Basically, the statute provides for a search warrant procedure to allow law enforcement intrusion into conversations and thereby seizing those conversations. Upon the request of the U.S. Attorney General or a specifically designated Assistant Attorney General, application may be made to a federal judge with competent jurisdiction for the issuance of an eavesdropping warrant. The application for the warrant must establish probable cause. The particular probable cause requirements for eavesdropping warrants are as follows:

1. That there is probable cause to believe someone is committing, has committed, or is about to commit a particular criminal act as specified in the law (offenses generally characterized as capital offenses or felonies, particularly those normally conducted by organized crime: bribery, bribery in sports contests, transmission of wagering information, embezzlement of pension and welfare frauds, drug transactions, fraud, etc).
2. That there is probable cause to believe that particular communications concerning the specified criminal activity will be obtained if the warrant and intrusion are granted.
3. That normal investigative procedures have been tried and have failed or reasonably appear to be unlikely to succeed or that they are too dangerous.
4. That there is probable cause to believe that the facilities from which or the place where the interception will take place are being used or are about to be used in connection with the commission of the specified criminal act and are leased to, listed in the name of, or commonly used by such persons.

In many respects the requirements for the eavesdropping warrant are far more stringent than those required for normal search warrants. Note that one requirement is the establishment of probable cause to believe that a particular conversation that has not yet taken place will take place and over a particularly specified phone. Note also that there must be a showing that other investigative methods have been tried and failed or are likely to fail. No such requirements exist for ordinary search warrants.

If a federal judge determines that probable cause exists to issue an eavesdropping warrant, the warrant will be issued authorizing a series of covert, surreptitious instrusions for up to thirty days (subject to extension and review by the judge). Progress reports may be required to insure against agent abuses, and conditions can be imposed upon the intrusive search. Following the termination of the intrusion, the taped conversations are sealed in a return made to the judge. Within a reasonable time thereafter, but not more than ninety days after termination of the period of the order or extensions thereof, the judge issuing the warrant causes notices to be issued to persons named in the order of application and such other parties to the intercepted communications as the judge determines should be notified. These notices must inform the persons of the following:

1. The fact of the entry of the order.
2. The date of the entry and the period of authorized, approved interception.
3. The fact that during the period, wire or oral communications were or were not intercepted.

A similar procedure for notice is provided in the event that an application is not approved. Access to the recordings may be granted by the judge. The recordings can be used in a federal or state court provided that certain notices are served upon the affected party ten days prior to trial.

There are certain exceptions to the requirements of the Act:

1. Interceptions by a party to a conversation who has consented to the intrusion.
2. Certain national security reasons.
3. Telephone company interceptions to safeguard against theft of its services.

The Act does not apply unless the *contents* of a warrant or oral communication are intercepted through the use of electronic, mechanical, or other similar devices. If conversations are heard with the naked ear, unaided by any electronic, mechanical, or similar device, the protections of the Act are inapplicable. If a *party* to a conversation agrees and consents to an interception by law enforcement agents, the Act also does not apply. If a conversation is not intercepted the Act does not apply. For example, often in organized crime investigations police officers will install or have installed "pen-registers" or "touch tone decoders," used to obtain the telephone number that is dialed or pushed on a telephone set, thereby learning who was calling whom. Such information is not a conversation and, as we shall see, not otherwise obtained under certain circumstances in violation of the Constitution or the Statute. In the case of *Smith v. Maryland*, 442 U.S. 735, the Court held that the installation and use of pen register devices were not searches and the detection of the numbers so dialed were not covered within any reasonable expectations or privacy.

The Wiretapping Act covers all forms of nonconsenual electronic or artificial interception of oral communication. Thus, electronic eavesdropping of a conversation between a group some distance away that cannot be heard with the naked, unaided ear is covered by the Act and its prohibitions.

Title III makes the unauthorized interception and disclosure of wire and oral communications a criminal act subject to fine and imprisonment. Title III authorizes state enactment of state wiretapping and electronic surveillance laws so long as the state laws are equal to or more restrictive than the federal law. About half of the states have enacted such legislation.

Authorization to wiretap or eavesdrop by electronic means is now constitutionally permissible provided the requirements of the Act or similar state laws are followed. The necessity for such authorizations with constitutional safeguards was recognized not only by the President's Crime Commission in 1967 but also was part of the specific finding of the Congressional Committee Report included in Title III:

> Organized criminals make extensive use of wire and oral communications in their criminal activities. The interception of such communications to obtain evidence of the commission of crimes to present their conversations is an indispensable aid to law enforcement and the administration of justice.[3]

Aside from Fourth Amendment issues presented in part as to organized crime matters, certain Fifth Amendment issues are of equal importance. As to particular organized crime investigations, there is an overlapping of the issues presented for determination, as we partly saw in the *Olmstead* case.

The Fifth Amendment provides in part:

> No person ... shall be compelled in any criminal case to be a witness against himself, nor be deprived of life, liberty, or property, without due process of law ...

Of particular importance to this discussion is the protection afforded within the Fifth Amendment as to incriminating statements: "No person ... shall be compelled in any criminal case to be a witness against himself ... " This is often referred to as the privilege against self-incrimination. Prior to 1936 not much Constitutional attention was given to this privilege. However, in 1936 the Supreme Court in *Brown v Mississippi*, 297 US 278 (1936) held that self-incriminating statements could not be used in a criminal trial if the defendant's confession was not voluntary and that the prosecution's attempted use of such a confession in state court was violative of the Fourteenth Amendment due process clause. Thirty years after *Brown, Miranda v Arizona*, 384 US 436 (1966), imposed certain obligations upon law enforcement officers seeking exculpatory statement from suspects. The Court held that prior to questioning a subject must be warned that he has a right to remain silent, that anything he says can be used against him in a court of law, that he has the right to the presence and advice of an attorney, and that if he cannot afford an attorney one will be appointed for him, free of charge, prior to questioning, if he so desires. The Court imposed these requirements upon law enforcement officers in addition to the voluntary requirements of *Brown v Mississippi* as to all custodial interrogations. Moreover, the Fifth and Fourteenth

---

[3]See P.L. No. 90-351, Section 801.

Amendment rules enunciated in *Brown* and *Miranda* only applied to confessions as communications, not to physical or tangible objects. For example, in electronic eavesdropping situations, normally, tape recordings are made of intercepted communications. When these conversations are played back in court, the prosecution is required to establish the speaker if it hopes to use the incriminating conversation. Often the speaker is established and identified by a person's testimony that the recording is the speaker's voice, when that person is familiar with that voice. Other times, such a match must be established through "voice print identification." Often that process requires that the defendant repeat certain recorded words so that an electronic print can be made of each and compared for similarities and upon that basis establish identification of the speaker through an expert opinion. In such situations, physical evidence is sought in the form of a voice print exemplar much like fingerprints or photographs. The provision of such voice print samples is subject to court order, and the Fifth Amendment constraints against compelling self-incrimination have no application inasmuch as physical evidence is sought rather than incriminating statements (*Schmerber v. California*, 384 US 757, 1966).

Many other Fifth Amendment issues arise in the course of the study of organized crime. To these we now turn. For example, in the case of *Massiah v. United States*, 337 U.S. 201 (1964), the U.S. Supreme Court considered the question of the admissibility of incriminating statements made by a defendant that were surreptitiously recorded by a government informant operating in conjunction with government law enforcement agents. The Court in determining whether or not such statements were admissible pursuant to the United States Constitution held that "[P]etitioners Fifth and Sixth Amendment rights were violated by the use of evidence against him of incriminating statements which government agents had deliberately elicited from him after he had been indicted [where such statements concerned the underlying facts of that indicted crime] and in the absence of retained counsel." The Court's decision principally focused upon the propriety of obtaining such statements through informants as to the underlying facts of the crime presently charged.

Two years later, the Court decided a related question in *Hoffa v*

United States, 385 U.S. 295 (1966), and reached a somewhat different conclusion than in the *Massiah* case. In *Hoffa*, the Court considered the admissibility of surreptitiously obtained incriminating statements made by Mr. Hoffa, a defendant in a then pending criminal trial. The statements, while not dealing with the matter for which he was then standing trial, dealt with Mr. Hoffa's alleged attempts to bribe members of the jury considering that criminal charge for which he was standing trial. The statements were obtained through the use of a government informant turned state's witness. The Court in considering the admissibility of these statements held that "[T]he Fourth Amendment [does not] protect a wrongdoer's misplaced belief that a person to whom he voluntarily confides his wrongdoing will not reveal it . . . [Since] no claim has been or could be made that [Hoffa's] . . . incriminating statements were the product of any sort of coercion, legal or factual, . . . it is clear that no right protected by the Fifth Amendment privilege against self-incrimination was violated in this case." The Court also found no violation of the Sixth Amendment right to counsel since eliciting the incriminating statements did not deal with the facts for which Hoffa was then standing trial.

Other Fifth Amendment issues often arise in the course of obtaining testimony from witnesses to be used in, *inter alia*, organized crime trials. Frequently, when such witnesses are called to testify, they claim and invoke the Fifth Amendment Privilege against self-incrimination and refuse to testify. Often, prosecutors must make decisions as to whether or not to seek grants of immunity as to such persons pursuant to Statute (see Chapters 14 and 15).

Three basic forms of witness immunity have developed:

1. *Use Immunity*—A grant of immunity from a prosecution based upon the actual testimony provided from the witness. However, if other evidence is developed, including any evidence derived from the actual testimony given, prosecution may proceed. In such a case, the actual testimony could not be used in such a proceeding.
2. *Use and Derivative Use Immunity*—A grant of immunity from a prosecution based upon the actual testimony provided from the witness and based upon any evidence derived from

that testimony. However, if evidence totally independent of the testimony provided and not derived from that testimony is obtained, prosecution may proceed. In such a case no actual testimony nor any evidence derived from that testimony, however, could be utilized in the prosecution.

3. *Transactional Immunity* — A grant of immunity from a prosecution for any criminal act that is mentioned by the subject during his testimony. In such a case no prosecution may take place for any criminal activity mentioned by the witness.

In situations where immunity is granted to a witness, the grant must be constitutionally co-extensive with the Fifth Amendment privilege that it replaces, or the witness cannot be compelled to answer incriminating questions. Once, however, a determination is made that the grant is equal to the privilege it replaces, then the jeopardy of answering is dissipated and a witness may be compelled by the court under threat of contempt to answer.

The United States Supreme Court has examined statutes pertaining to immunity in some significant cases:

1. *Counselman v Hitchcock,* 142 US 547 (1892): This case declared *Use Immunity Statutes* unconstitutional inasmuch as this grant of immunity is not co-extensive with the privilege it replaces.

2. *Brown v Walker,* 161 US 591 (1896): This case determined *Transactional Immunity* statutes were constitutional because the statutory grant of immunity was equal to the privilege it replaced.

3. *Kastigar v United States,* 406 US 441 (1972): The Court in this case, despite certain *dicta* in the *Counselman* case (to the effect that only transactional immunity statutes would be permissible), held that use and derivative use statutes leave the "witness and the prosecutorial authorization in substantially the same position as if the witness had claimed the Fifth Amendment privilege. The immunity is therefore co-extensive with the privilege and suffers to supplant it."[4]

---

[4]*Kastigar v United States,* 406 US 441 (1972).

As we shall discuss in Chapter 14, the actual immunity granted and the procedure involved takes some time and often constant effort.

Often related to Fourth and Fifth Amendment cases like *Hoffa* and *Osborn*, are cases involving claims of government entrapment. Entrapment claims are often put forth in organized crime cases as affirmative defenses to criminal charges. Such defenses require, in essence, admission of the act and then the use of the government's improper conduct as a defense. There are certain requirements necessary for the proper operation of the defense best exemplified by an examination of the cases presented in Chapter 11.

Aside from issues arising as a result of the protections afforded by the Fourth and Fifth Amendments, sometimes including the Fourteenth Amendment as well (primarily as to state action), other particular issues arise as a result of efforts put forth to criminalize organized criminal conduct as a criminal act. Recall from Chapter 1 the problems that have arisen in simply defining organized crime, remember Senator McClellan's efforts to do so for the purposes of drafting federal criminal statutes to outlaw membership in La Cosa Nostra, and then consider the enormous difficulty in drafting statutes useful and necessary for organized crime prosecutions that meet minimum constitutional due process standards of clarity and fairness.

In 1926 the Supreme Court succinctly stated the rule for criminal statute constitutional clarity in *Connally v. General Construction Co.*, 269 US 385 (1926):

> The terms of a penal statute . . . must be sufficiently explicit to inform those who are subject to it what conduct on their part will render them liable to its penalties is a well-recognized requirement, consonant alike with ordinary motives of fair play and the settled rules of law: and a statute which otherwise forbids or requires the doing of an act in terms so vague that men of common intelligence must necessarily guess at its meaning and differ as to its application violates the first essential of due process of law.

The federal R.I.C.O. statute, examined in Chapter 7, has passed this constitutional test. However, some state efforts to define and proscribe organized criminal conduct have not been as successful. Ohio in 1974 passed a new criminal statute designed to make active participation in an organized crime enterprise as defined a felony of the first degree. The statute in 1980 was examined by the state's highest court and ultimately declared unconstitutional based upon concepts synonymous with those principles laid down in the *Connally* case (see *State v. Young*, 62 Ohio St. 2d 370, 1980).

Constitutional issues abound in the study of the enforcement of organized crime. The student must be keenly aware of all of the doctrines and of the possible problems, not only those pointed out in this chapter but also those pointed out throughout the book.

CHAPTER 10

DEVELOPMENT OF AN INTELLIGENCE SYSTEM

The President's 1967 *Report* recommended the establishment of intelligence units to investigate, gather, analyze, and disseminate information about organized crime. The Commission specifically recommended the creation of such units in state attorney general's offices as well as prosecuting attorneys' offices and police departments in all major United States cities. The Commission also recommended federal assistance for computer storage and dissemination of intelligence information about organized crime.[1]

These recommendations have been followed to a degree by federal, state, and local government. The Department of Justice through the now defunct L.E.A.A. (Law Enforcement Assistance Administration) did provide funds to assist in the development of systems for intelligence gathering and analysis. These systems have been deployed within many jurisdictions, although the Commission recommendations as to the establishment of regional intelligence systems and a centralized, computerized system into which all information could be put have not come about as quickly nor as easily as the funding for intelligence system development.

Regional networks for information exchange among agencies have been developed. Most recently the Mid-Atlantic–Great Lakes Organized Crime Law Enforcement Network (MAGLOCLEN) was founded for an eight-state region, which almost completes a national system of regional information networks,[2] as recommended by the President's 1967 Commission.

---

[1]The President's Commission on Law Enforcement and Administration of Justice, *The Challenge of Crime in a Free Society: A Report*, p. 204 (Washington D.C., 1967).

[2]*See* Pennsylvania Crime Commission, *A Decade of Organized Crime: 1980 Report*, pp. 12–13 (St. Davids, Penna. 1980).

There is now universal agreement that a law enforcement intelligence system is a necessary prerequisite to any effective effort to combat organized crime. The Justice Department through L.E.A.A. funded the preparation and publication of *Basic Elements of Intelligence: A Manual of Theory, Structures and Procedures for Use By Law Enforcement Agencies Against Organized Crime.* This intelligence manual, published in 1971 and authored by E. Drexel Godfrey, Jr., Ph.D., and Don R. Harris, Ph.D., has become the leading authority on this subject area. Much of this chapter and the following three are based upon information provided therein.

An intelligence system is basically the process by which information fed into the system is converted into judgments, descriptions, or conclusions, which are in turn used to further achieve certain specific purposes only one of which is prosecution in the organized crime setting. Over the years, far too much emphasis has been placed upon the development of information for use solely in prosecution of particular organized crime figures. Such approaches are really evidence gathering functions and have little to do with real intelligence gathering or analysis activities. If such approaches are followed, the "blinders" created in the process will screen out much useful information that could in turn assist in the development of more important overall strategies to be deployed against organized crime as an ongoing criminal phenomena.

For example, if this approach had been followed by the McClellan Subcommittee, most of the otherwise useful information provided by Joseph Valachi would have been deemed irrelevant and therefore excluded. Much of Mr. Valachi's revelations about La Cosa Nostra would not and could not, for example, be revealed in a criminal trial. The President's 1967 Crime Commission in this regard made the following findings:

> At present, most law enforcement agencies gather organized crime intelligence information with prosecution as the immediate objective. This tactical focus has not been accomplished by development of the full potential for strategic intelligence. That failure accounts for the gaps in knowledge ... concerning the ways in which criminal cartels organize and operate as a business. Prosecution based merely upon individual violations that come to the attention of law enforcement may result in someone's

incarceration, but the criminal organization simply places someone else in the vacated position.[3]

The development of information beyond these immediately obvious goals is clearly necessary. The development of such intelligence occurs as a result of higher and more important goals and objectives of the intelligence system.

The intelligence system really resembles a factory of sorts where raw materials (basic information) are processed by conversion of those materials into goods for the marketplace. Intelligence, itself, is really the end product of a complex process, which is almost always an informed judgment. The process that generates these judgments is the "intelligence process." The process is both investigative and fact generating as well as effective in the analysis of organized crime.

There are two basic types of intelligence information as identified by the President's Commission and analyzed in Godfrey and Harris:

1. *Tactical Intelligence* — Information that is obtained for immediate law enforcement objectives, such as specific organized crime prosecutions.

2. *Strategic Intelligence* — Information that is the highest end product of the intelligence system. Information that is used to assess the capabilities, intentions, and vulnerabilities of organized crime groups. It is a major aspect of the development of overall enforcement strategies and future planning. Information that has developed about the interworkings of La Cosa Nostra is an example of this type of intelligence.[4]

By far the most important intelligence in the long run is strategic in nature:

> The body of strategic intelligence information would enable agencies to predict what directions organized crime might take, which industries it might try to penetrate, and how it might infiltrate. Law enforcement and regulatory agencies could then develop plans to destroy the organizational framework and coherence of the criminal cartels. Comprehensive strategic planning, however, even with an expanded intelligence effort,

---

[3]*Report, supra*, note 1 at 199.

[4]See E. D. Godfrey, Jr., & D. Harris, *Basic Elements of Intelligence* (Washington D.C. 1971).

will not be possible until relevant disciplines, such as economics, political science, sociology, and operations research, begin to study organized crime intensively.[5]

At the heart of any intelligence system is an intelligence unit. The size, responsibilities, diversity of personnel, resources, and similar basics of such a unit are largely determined by the size of the overall agency the unit serves and the amount of funds available to that agency. However, no matter what the size, every intelligence unit must have three essential components:

1. *Information Files*—In larger units this information would be computer fed and stored while in smaller units it would be manually filed and held. In either case, however, it must be properly referenced and labeled, cross-referenced, indexed, and organized to obtain maximum functional utilization of the information.
2. *Permanent Informational Flow System*—A permanent, formal system that is fact generating must be employed for the unit. Information about public as well as private sources must be tapped for input into this system.
3. *Analysis of Information*—At the very center of any intelligence unit sits those persons responsible for the conversion of raw information into usable data: the analysts. This central conversion of information process is perhaps the most important part of the system, as it converts raw facts into usable intelligence.

The intelligence process is composed of nine basic parts:

1. Information Collection.
2. Information Evaluation.
3. Information Collation.
4. Information Analysis.
5. Reporting of Information.
6. Dissemination of Information.
7. Reevaluation of Information.
8. Management.
9. Use of Information.

---

[5]*Report, supra,* Notel, at 199.

The process is depicted in Figure 5. Each step or part may be defined as follows:

1. *Collection:* Gathering of raw information from public as well as private sources for eventual use in the system (see Chapter 11). Collection involves the use of both *overt* (open) and *covert* (secretive) collection activities and methods.
2. *Evaluation:* Assessing the value of information obtained for input into the intelligence system by rating both its factual validity and its source validity through an assessment of source reliability (see Chapter 11).
3. *Collation:* Sifting, sorting, storing, indexing, and cross-referencing of information for later recall (see Chapter 12).
4. *Analysis:* An analytical process by which information is converted into intelligence. Information is put in a logical form, examined, questions are asked, and upon that basis a hypothesis is developed and tested for accuracy. Many analysis tools are used (see Chapter 12).
5. *Reporting:* Written end product of intelligence information developed as a result of collection, evaluation, collation, and analysis efforts, i.e., an end product of the system.
6. *Dissemination:* Transmittal of the reporting function to appropriate components within or without the agency (see Chapter 13).
7. *Reevaluation:* Use of information developed as a result of the intelligence process to determine effectiveness of reporting, deployment of personnel, and the overall efficiency and responsiveness of the system (see Chapter 13).
8. *Management:* Use of information developed to manage the unit, e.g., evaluation of personnel and the end product.
9. *Utilization of Information:* Although perhaps not as a strict matter a direct part of the intelligence system per se, the information generated by the system is used by others, for example, to prosecute. Prosecutorial efforts within the criminal justice system, including the use of grand juries, generate facts that are returned to the intelligence system. Thus, the use of information created by the system in turn frequently generates more information for use within the system;

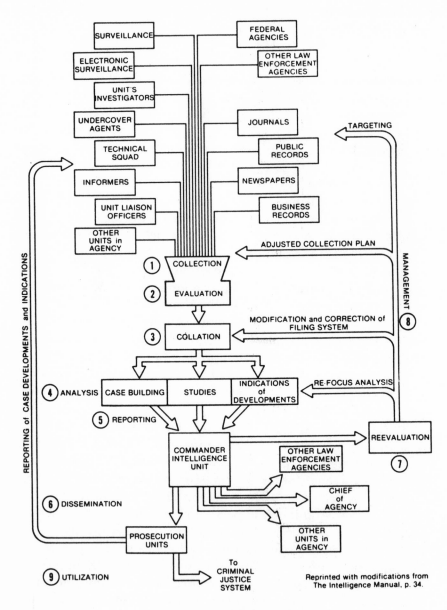

Figure 5. The intelligence process.

what is generated is again used to generate more information completing the evolutionary circle of the process (see Chapters 13, 14, 15, and 16).

The formulation of intelligence systems to assist in the development of overall strategies to combat organized crime is becoming far more commonplace than fifteen years ago. Since the 1967 *President's Report*, much has been learned about the various aspects of organized crime. That educational process has in turn assisted in the recognition of the weaknesses of organized crime groups, which are finally being penetrated with much success. For example, this learning process has certainly assisted in the FBI's recent successful penetration of Mafia crime groups by an FBI agent who spent some six years undercover penetrating the Bonanno La Cosa Nostra crime family. Not only was intelligence undoubtedly used to select the right agent to go underground but it was also used to determine which group to penetrate and where and when to start, and most importantly the intelligence theretofore gathered certainly gave the agent enough information to adapt a much different and yet correct life-style for his undercover work. Without prior intelligence gathering, such a penetration would have been impossible.

The increased utilization of intelligence systems by police agencies has not been universally acclaimed despite strong recommendations of the President's 1967 Crime Commission. There seems to be a real fear in some of the development of such systems with accompanying intelligence activities largely due to the *aggressive* or *prospective* nature of law enforcement efforts in this regard.

Historically and traditionally, law enforcement efforts to deal with crime (including organized crime) have been responsive or reactive. Eventually, it became apparent that such activities and methods while perhaps effective in catching a robber or solving a murder could not be even slightly effective with more sophisticated crime groups. As a consequence, recommendations such as those made by the President's 1967 Crime Commission were taken up and implemented by many enforcement agencies. Unfortunately such enforcement efforts have upon occasion been abused. Abuses of prospective enforcement efforts including the collection and accumulation of personal data, surveillance, electronic surveillance, and undercover operations can all impinge to varying degrees upon personal liberties.

The criticisms directed against such efforts include the following:

> During the gathering of intelligence, much information of a type which is considered private will be obtained concerning people who have committed no crime . . .
>
> More than the fact of [intelligence information] . . . collection, the analysis methods applied to the information gathered by intelligence activities conflict with the idea of a limited reactive police force. What a broad intelligence system is looking for—what its computers can find—are *patterns*, mainly patterns of association. [Techniques to develop evidence of those patterns are] . . . powerful technique[s], yielding a great deal of extremely valuable information, but also posing a real danger of misuse. . . .
>
> Even when used totally in good faith, strategic intelligence violates basic privacy concepts in three ways. First, the type of information it requires is not only drawn from public records which are not ordinarily combined, but it is also material which is generally considered private. Second, the basic analytical tool is guilt by association. . . . Finally, it vests huge discretion in the investigators as to what information to gather and how to analyze it and use it.[6]

Moreover, arguments against surveillance, electronic eavesdropping, and the employment of tracking devices have permeated legal and lay literature. Abuses have occurred, but it is imperative that the intelligence system and its accompanying activities continue to develop if any real effort against organized crime is to be made. Furthermore, it is essential to keep the intelligence system and its activities in perspective. For example, the use of analysis methods to develop "patterns of association" are not employed to find "guilt by association" but rather for the purposes of developing a hypothesis as to the basic supposed composition and structure of a given organized crime group. Once the analysis method is used to develop the hypothesis, it must be subjected to testing to confirm or disprove the elements of the hypothesis. Only after that testing process has been completed would any conclusions as to organizational structure, composition, or associations of a group be drawn. Therefore, this fear at least is misplaced.

---

[6]Applegate, "The Business Papers Rule: Personal Privacy and White Collar Crime," *16 Akron Law Review*, 189, 194–6, (Fall 1982) (footnotes omitted).

Expressed fears as to the collection of public information by intelligence units are even more perplexing to a degree. How can there be any real potential for abuse when information is gathered from open sources? Perhaps the real fear stems from the actual combination of such information or the mere fact that all such information can be collected rather than what is collected. In any case, intelligence activities cannot be totally effective unless all information, including factual data and other nonincriminating factors, is considered and assessed. Moreover, the potentials for abuse as to information obtained from open, public sources is far less subject to abuse than potential abuse due to information acquisition from covert operations.

Some concern has also been expressed as to potential "chilling" effects that association pattern analysis techniques may create upon First Amendment rights to freedom of association in addition to general privacy considerations.[7] The claim is that persons will be less likely to meet and associate with others (as is their constitutional right) because of interference with such persons' rights to maintain a degree of secrecy as to their personal associations and relationships.[8]

In a case before the Supreme Court in 1957, *N.A.A.C.P. v Alabama*, 357 U.S. 499 (1957), the Court in examining First Amendment rights to association held that "[I]mmunity from state scrutiny of [lawful associations] . . . is . . . so related to the right of the members to pursue their lawful private interest privately and to associate freely with others in so doing as to come within the protections of the Fourteenth Amendment."

Despite the Court's holding, however, it should be noted that the Court drew clear distinctions between the interests of *lawful* private groups and the intents of similar *unlawful* groups. While the former's activities and membership lists were subject to First and Fourteenth Amendment protections so as to preserve their right to free association, the latter groups were not so protected due to the "particular character of [their] . . . activities, involving

---

[7]*Id.* at 204–205.

[8]See Hufstedler, *The Directions and Misdirections of a Constitutional Right to Privacy*, 26 Rec. A.B. City N.Y. 546, 558 (1971).

acts of unlawful intimidation and violence . . . ." Such distinctions clearly apply as to investigations of organized crime members and their associations through membership in a variety of criminal cartels. In fact, it would seem appropriate perhaps if a "chilling" effect on these illicit associations would take place as a result of intelligence activities.

Such clear distinctions, however, that can be drawn as between such groups as the N.A.A.C.P. and La Cosa Nostra become much more difficult to make as the character of the organization becomes less distinct. Such an issue arose in another case argued before the United States Supreme Court some fifteen years after the *N.A.A.C.P. v. Alabama* decision. This case, *Laird v. Tatum*, 408 U.S. 1 (1972), concerned the effect of an existing intelligence system as to whether or not the mere existence of such a system amounted to an impermissible chilling agent upon the constitutionally protected right to association.

Although the Court avoided the rendition of a direct opinion as to the propriety of the Army's detailed intelligence activities, the Court did conclude that the mere existence of an enforcement intelligence system engaging in monitoring and surveillance activities did not *in and of itself* create a chilling effect upon any constitutional right of association. Absent a claim of "specific [and] present objective harm or a threat of specific future harm," the Court reasoned that a case for resolution by the courts is not presented.

Results similar to the *Laird* opinion have been reached by several lower courts. Often, these cases have had to deal with subtle distinctions in fact patterns under review when compared to prior case precedents. One of these cases, dealing with such distinctions, was decided two years after the *Laird* case. The decision reached by the United States Court of Appeals for the Second Circuit in *The Fifth Avenue Peace Parade Committee v. Gray*, 480 F.2d 326 (1973), involved in part an examination of a different intelligence operation (and conducted by the F.B.I. of organizers of an antiwar demonstration) as well as of different intelligence data accrued in the course of the operation, (public information direct from open sources as well as private information derived from a certain bank record of an organizer). The Court of Appeals found as to the F.B.I.'s intelligence operation proof "beyond a reasonable doubt" of "legitimate" interest in the activities of the targeted group and even countenanced their prospective rather than reactionary enforcement efforts.[9] The Court of Appeals moreover did not make any real distinction from the *Laird* case because of the F.B.I.'s acquisition of a private bank record in the course of its intelligence operation.

Both the *Laird* decision and the *Gray* case also dealt with questions surrounding the Army's and the F.B.I.'s dissemination of intelligence information to other agencies. Both decisions ultimately concluded that no chilling effect per se arose from this mere dissemination of such information absent a showing of specific harm.

A review of these decisions should assist in dispelling those fears of intelligence systems and their operations previously cited. All of these opinions clearly involved groups with more legitimate societal interests than organized crime groups. Several specific conclusions from these cases can be derived as to intelligence systems and their operations and activities:

1. First and Fourteenth Amendment protections of association are extended to private groups engaged in *lawful* as opposed to *unlawful* activities.
2. The mere existence of intelligence systems engaged in monitoring, surveillance, and similar activities does not create a chilling effect upon any constitutional right of association in and of itself.
3. Prospective rather than reactive law enforcement efforts are often necessary and entirely appropriate.
4. The acquisition of private intelligence data along with more public data does not create an unwarranted intrusion into group association unless it involves an otherwise constitutionally protected area.
5. The dissemination or sharing of intelligence data among enforcement agencies does not create a chilling effect upon association activities in and of itself.

---

[9]*Fifth Avenue Peace Parade Committee v. Gray*, 480 F.2d 326,332 (2nd Cir., 1973).

Intelligence operations as we have seen are extremely important to any overall enforcement response to the problem of organized crime. Such operations are not, despite some expressed fears, unlawful or unconstitutional. While abuses in such systems have occurred and may occur in the future, society's interests in combating organized crime should outweigh these fears and the small potentials for abuse.

Chapter 11

COLLECTION AND EVALUATION
OF INFORMATION

The real life's blood of any effective intelligence system and, for that matter, any effective response to the threat of organized crime is information that must be *current, accurate,* and *useful.* The acquisition and flow of information into an intelligence unit for eventual analysis cannot be haphazard if the process is to be effective. The production of information is really part of the circuitous overall intelligence process inasmuch as it feeds the process as well as helps direct its future collection activities. The information acquired today, once analyzed, helps determine the focus as to what new information is needed. The collection process, while fact generating, becomes fact seeking after the needs for new information are recognized.

Information to be collected and directed into the intelligence system can come from a variety of sources. Some of these sources are so obvious that it is initially difficult to imagine how certain information could possibly assist any law enforcement investigative effort. Such information standing alone might be meaningless; however, once all such information is combined and analyzed its overall usefulness becomes apparent.

Collection activities focus on the acquisition of information through *both* overt methods and sources and covert methods and sources. Each category of information and each information acquisition method can provide valuable information on organized crime.

There are four basic types of intelligence information when studying collection activities:

1. *Indicative Intelligence Information:* Information suggesting new developments or trends in organized crime structures.

131

2. *Strategic Intelligence Information:* Intelligence that is of the highest order. Information collected over time, to be put together, and analyzed to indicate patterns of organized crime activity.
3. *Tactical Intelligence Information:* Information for which there is an immediate need and use, which is usually turned over to active enforcement units for follow up.
4. *Evidential Intelligence Information:* Information that is factual, precise, and admissible for use in court proceedings.

Such intelligence information is acquired through one of two general sources or methods: *overt* and *covert*. There are five overt sources for intelligence information gathering:

1. Intraagency Law Enforcement Units;
2. Other Law Enforcement Agencies;
3. Public Officers;
4. Businesses, Corporations, and Trade Associations; and
5. Newspapers, Journals, and Magazine Publishers.

There are four *covert* methods of intelligence information gathering or sources for such information:

1. Surveillance, including employment of "tracking devices," i.e., beepers;
2. Electronic surveillance and wiretapping;
3. Informants; and
4. Undercover operations.

Although other sources can provide information for the intelligence system, such as reports of investigative grand juries and public or quasipublic crime commissions, these nine sources or methods of intelligence information gathering are the most frequently used inputs for the intelligence system. An examination of each collection method or source and activity will be helpful in achieving an overall understanding of the collection and evaluation process.

Information and information sources within any police department or law enforcement agency already can provide valuable touchstones for information. It is extremely important, however, if such sources are to be used that they understand that no information will be used for any internal affairs operations but rather will be used for organized crime intelligence investigations. Once that understanding is made, much information within the agency can be readily acquired.

Within most law enforcement agencies, several different units are quite readily available for information acquisition:

1. Road or Traffic Patrol Units;
2. Homicide Units;
3. Vice Units;
4. Narcotics Units;
5. Robbery or Theft Units; and
6. Miscellaneous Enforcement Units.

The information acquired from each such unit can often be valuable in the collection process for any intelligence system. Monthly or weekly meetings with members of each unit can keep the information flowing to the intelligence unit for evaluation, storage, and analysis. Cooperation between regular enforcement units and an intelligence unit is extremely important to the information collection process. Such units frequently come into contact every day with a wide variety of subjects, and their observations of a multitude of activities can help in developing not only information but also an overall picture of organized criminal activity.

Information from the regular enforcement units should be passed on through the use of a permanent report form identifying particular information, e.g., targeted individuals, contacts, cars, license plate numbers, observed meetings, etc. The report form should include the date and time, reporting officer, identifying badge number or unit, locations involved, and any other important information as to the observed activity. Information thus recorded can be further refined through personal contacts with the reporting officer by an intelligence unit analyst if necessary.

Aside from the use of regular report forms, intelligence unit collectors may often engage in debriefing activities of individual officers to glean if possible important information regarding particular enforcement activities. Debriefing might be defined as the systematic questioning of a person about an observed activity or event with the objective of obtaining more specific and useful information from that person about that activity or event. Often, debriefing activities occur after other enforcement units' investigations of given activities. Such efforts sometimes lead to valuable intelligence information. Regular and thorough reviews of other units' reports assist in the selection of individual officers for debriefing.

Other law enforcement agencies at all governmental levels can prove to be a valuable source for intelligence input. Some restrictions created by statute, administrative regulation, or constitutional considerations often limit the free and ready exchange of organized crime information between law enforcement agencies, see Chapters 9 and 13.

The President's Crime Commission emphasized the need for such exchanges in its 1967 *Report*:

> Since the activities of organized crime overlap individual police jurisdictions, the various law enforcement agencies must share information and coordinate their plans.
>
> On the Federal level, enforcement agencies are furnishing a large amount of intelligence to the Organized Crime and Racketeering (OCR) Section in the Department of Justice. But there is no central place where a strategic intelligence system regarding organized crime groups is being developed to coordinate an integrated Federal plan for enforcement and regulatory agencies.
>
> Regional law enforcement organizations should be developed to "permit and encourage greater exchange of information among Federal, State and local agencies."[1]

Despite such recommendations, progress toward a greater exchange of information has been somewhat limited. Various privacy acts and other federal and state legislation have greatly hampered a more liberal exchange of information. Moreover, information exchange has been inhibited at all governmental levels between departments. For example, federal prosecutors are greatly limited by federal statute in obtaining information from the Internal Revenue Service among other agencies. Although some regulation may be necessary, such regulations have greatly restricted the free flow of organized crime intelligence data between agencies.

---

[1]The President's Commission on Law Enforcement and Administration of Justice, *Crime in a Free Society: A Report*, pp. 204, 206 (Washington D.C., 1967).

Aside from certain legal restrictions sometimes inhibiting the flow of information, mistrust, political differences, and even petty jealousies often prevent the free flow of information. Law enforcement historically has been composed of various diverse local personalities with varying professional degrees of competence. Many have been or are subject to corruption, and as a consequence interagency cooperation has been limited and, in such instances, properly so.

The designation within departments of information or liaison officers often can assist in the exchange of information between agencies. Relationships between such specially appointed officers can greatly nurture the development of respect, trust, and cooperation between the officers and their agencies. Membership within local, state, or regional information exchanges also can greatly assist in the development of respect and trust among agencies.

Aside from information exchanged within or between law enforcement agencies, various public offices are depositories for very valuable yet totally public information. The data available at local and state levels can be initially surprising to the intelligence officer. The following are very valuable sources of intelligence information for organized crime investigations:

1. *Information About Real Property:*
    a. Recorder's Office.
    b. Building Departments.
    c. Fire Departments, Health Departments, Zoning Offices, Street Departments.
    d. Auditor's and Treasurer's Offices.
2. *Information About Personal Property:*
    a. Auditor's and Treasurer's Offices.
    b. Recorder's Office.
    c. Motor Vehicle Registrars or Title Officers.
    d. Probate Court.
    e. Courts.
3. *Information Sources of Personal Information:*
    a. Courts.
    b. Recorder's Office.

    c. Permit Offices.
4. *Municipal and Local Governmental Records.*
5. *State Offices:*
    a. Secretary of State's Office.
    b. Attorney General's Office.
    c. Securities Division or Department.
    d. Banking Division or Department.
    e. Legislative Services.
    f. Miscellaneous State Departments.
6. *Federal Offices.*

PRIVACY STATUTES, FREEDOM OF
INFORMATION, AND PUBLIC RECORD LAWS

The collection of information, primarily from other public agencies, has been hampered to a degree and certainly confused by the enactment of a plethora of federal and state legislation. Most of this legislation has dealt with the creation and protection of various rights to privacy; however, some has sought to maintain a degree of public access to information about our governments. In the end, however, the legislation (while frequently exempting law enforcement information from the nondisclosure constraints of the privacy acts and also exempting such information from being classified as public under freedom of information acts) has created havoc among the agencies. Various interpretations of such laws (and regulations promulgated thereunder) as well as the constant and ever-increasing threat of lawsuits have made enforcement agencies wary of both disclosure and nondisclosure. As a consequence the free flow of information, the collection of information, and the recommendations of the 1967 President's Crime Commission have been hampered in the process.

As we discussed in Chapter 9 and as set out in Chapter 13, much of this legislation, while good intentioned, has greatly hurt organized crime investigations. While some legislation has been designed to assist such investigations, the vast majority of the legislation has hampered such efforts. One notable exception to this basic proposition is the so-called Bank Secrecy Act.[2] The law, enacted in 1970, was passed to assist "law enforcement authorities . . . [in the acquisition of] greater evidence of financial transactions in order to reduce the incidence of white collar crime."[3] Congress specifically found in Section 1829 b(a) of the Act that "adequate records maintained by insured banks have a high degree of usefulness in criminal . . . investigations."[4]

This Act, part of the Bank Records and Foreign Transactions Act, P.L. 91-508, requires the maintenance of certain bank records under regulations prescribed by the Secretary of the Treasury. These rules require banks to keep microfilm or similar reproductive records of checks, drafts, and similar negotiable instruments as well as records regarding the identity of persons holding accounts. Another part of this law requires the reporting of cash currency transactions by banks if the payment or receipt involves cash of $10,000 or more; this amount was set by the Secretary of the Treasury pursuant to regulations enacted under the law.[5] This latter measure, as we discussed in Chapter 7, was primarily designed to assist in drug investigations.

Although the Act was almost immediately challenged after its passage, the Supreme Court in *California Bankers Association v Schultz*, 416 U.S. 21 (1974), upheld its constitutionality and recognized the Act's importance to law enforcement. There can be little question of the Act's usefulness to law enforcement officers seeking information as to complex financial transactions. In 1978, however, Congress enacted the Right to Financial Privacy Act of 1978.[6] Generally, the law, while perhaps good intentioned, makes it more difficult for law enforcement officers to obtain information from bank records as to financial transactions of suspected organized crime members among others. Information kept by banks pursuant to the Bank Secrecy Act can still be obtained, but pursu-

---

[2]P. L. 91-508, Sec. 101 *et seq.*, 84 Stat. 1114 (1970) now contained in 12 U.SC. Sec. 18296 (1970).

[3]S. Rep. No. 1139, 91st Cong., 2d Sess. 1 (1970). See also H. R. Rep. No. 975, 91st Cong., 2nd Sess. 10 (1970).

[4]12 U.S.C. Sec. 1829b (a).

[5]See P.L. 91-508 Sec. 221 *et seq.* (1970). See also 31 U.S.C. Sec. 1051 (1970).

[6]Pub. L. No. 95-630, 92 Stat. 3697 (1978). Now codified in 12 U.S.C. Sec. 3401 *et seq.*

ant to the terms of the Financial Privacy Act, a search warrant, subpoena duces tecum, customer's consent, or formal written request is necessary absent very limited emergency circumstances.

Aside from the information acquisition restrictions created by the morass of federal and state privacy and information legislation, further state and federal information is sometimes excluded from public (and law enforcement) review based upon claims of executive or legislative privilege or national security. Such claims are often recognized by the courts, and as a consequence some information is just not discoverable by law enforcement officers.

Aside from the voluminous wealth of publicly collected and available information to law enforcement officers engaged in organized crime investigations, much relevant useful information can be obtained from media sources. Investigative reporters often provide valuable, current, and relevant information regarding organized crime figures and their activities. The importance of such efforts in the war against organized crime has even been recognized by the President's Crime Commission.[7]

Newspapers, magazines, trade publications, professional journals, and television and radio coverage transcripts are often very valuable sources of information. General interest magazines, particularly *Newsweek, US News and World Report, Time, Forbes,* and some other publications, provide fresh and current synopses of organized crime trends and current individual organized crime principals all over the country and the world.

Much valuable media information is available in most university and public libraries, especially in larger metropolitan areas. Information on file in such libraries is usually indexed so it can be readily withdrawn. *The New York Times Index* and certain other major newspaper indices can be used to locate and identify by subject matter articles about organized crime activities or figures. Key word selection is the mainstay of locating information in such indices.

Magazines are also indexed by subject matter in the *Reader's Guide to Periodical Literature.* Other trade publications or professional journals also have similar indices that can be used to locate

---

[7] *Report, supra,* note 1 at 208.

many detailed and in-depth articles about organized crime. Once located through the use of such indices, useful information can be gleaned and put into the intelligence system.

Many records kept by various, mainly publicly held, companies are often available to the general public. Typically, information in this category would include yearly financial statements, as well as reports to shareholders. More detailed information can sometimes be obtained if information is requested and obtained through a shareholder of the corporation who would have certain statutory rights to access to the books and records of that corporation, its shareholder's names, addresses, and holdings, and many other facts about the business. Often such information can be obtained from trade or business associations such as the Better Business Bureau, The Chamber of Commerce, and others having individualized associations of businessmen or various tradesmen.

Information collected through the acquisition of intelligence data from open sources, once fed into the intelligence system, can provide valuable background information, especially important to further investigative targeting efforts as well as the development of strategic intelligence. For example, information from public sources regarding a particular organized crime individual can certainly assist in selecting and directing covert collection activities designed to "fill the holes" left after a review of public source information.

COVERT OPERATIONS

Perhaps the most effective law enforcement intelligence gathering activity occurs during the course of conducting covert intelligence gathering operations. Covert collection actions may be defined as "the acquisition of information from a subject who is unaware he is being observed or overheard, although he may suspect that he is a target."[8]

Covert collection methods must often be used to gain more accurate insights into the everyday workings of organized crime groups. It is clearly necessary and essential if any evidence is to be

---

[8]E. D. Godfrey, and R. D. Harris, *Basic Elements of Intelligence*, p. 19 (Washington D.C., 1971).

gathered for ultimate use in the development of strategic intelligence or in any organized crime prosecution. An examination of each such method is essential to any complete understanding of the effective investigation of organized crime.

Surveillance

Surveillance is the most common of the covert intelligence collection activities. Surveillance is the observation, monitoring, and tracking, if necessary, of suspects who are unaware of the monitoring activity. Some authorities have defined it as "the *secretive* and *continuous* watching of persons, places or objects to obtain information concerning the activities and identities of individuals."[9] Surveillance is typically of two types: *stationary*, which is conducted from a concealed, fixed location as to another location so as to observe and record the comings and goings and activities taking place at that latter location; and *moving*, which is when one or more agents proceed from location to location following the targeted subject or subjects in an effort to observe and monitor the associations of the subject with other persons and locations as well as the activities of that subject.

Surveillance has definite limitations even though several methods have been developed. For example, while the technique is sometimes successful in learning patterns and movements, associations with other individuals or places, or clandestine meetings, it is almost always unsuccessful in learning what the meetings are about, what is said, or what is planned. Consequently, the method must often be supplemented with other covert intelligence gathering activities to confirm or disprove the tentative conclusions frequently drawn by intelligence analysts as to the surveillance derived intelligence data.

Often during the course of surveillance operations, photographic or video recordings are made of the officers' observations, particularly when stationary surveillance is employed. Such records are often used in subsequent court proceedings.

The objects of surveillance activities are:

---

[9]Ohio Organized Crime Prevention Council, "*Systems One*—1975 *Organized Crime Seminar,* "Surveillance Technique Section," P. 1 (1975).

A. To obtain evidence of a crime.
B. To locate persons by watching their haunts and associates.
C. To obtain detailed information about a subjects' activities.
D. To check on the reliability of informants.
E. To locate hidden property or contraband.
F. To obtain probable cause for obtaining search warrants, [arrest warrants, wiretaps, or other electronic surveillance].
G. To prevent the commission of an act or to apprehend a subject in the commission of an act.
H. To obtain information for later use in interrogation.
I. To develop leads and information received from other sources.
J. To know at all times the whereabouts of an individual.
K. To obtain admissible *legal evidence* for use in court.
[L. To learn of associations and determine organizational groupings and patterns].[10]

There are three basic moving surveillance methods:

1. *One-Man Foot or Vehicle Surveillance* (one officer following the subject): One-man surveillance methods are very difficult and the most susceptible to discovery because of the need to maintain a rather close distance to the subject in order to monitor his movements properly.

2. *Two-Man Foot or Vehicle Surveillance (AB Method)* (two officers following the subject): The use of two agents to conduct a surveillance allows for greater surveillance flexibility. Distances between the subject and the officers can be greater, and the point or lead officer can be switched and alternated between the agents to lessen the chances of detection, which is commonly called "leap-frogging." Two different vantage points can also be used to ensure greater accuracy of observation while decreasing the chances of detection.

3. *Three Man Foot or Vehicle Surveillance (ABC Method)* (three officers following the subject): Increased accuracy of surveillance and decreased risk of detection flow with the use of this method. Like the AB Method, leap frogging between the three agents can lessen the chances of discovery. If radio equipment can be used by the agents, one or two agents can follow a parallel route, and if the subject turns left or right, he

---

[10]*Id* (from Michigan Department of State Police, Intelligence Section).

or she can be readily picked up by the parallel route agent while the prior point agent proceeds to the next available parallel route and takes that route, to again pick up the subject on a subsequent turn.[11]

Various methods are often used by subjects to guard against and detect surveillance. Consequently, agents engaged in such activities must be constantly alert to blend into the surroundings as much as possible and to act as normal as possible. The use of beepers attached to a subject or his vehicle greatly increases the distance over which a subject may be tracked, although such use is subject to certain possible constitutional constraints (see Chapter 9).

Electronic Surveillance and Wiretapping

The effectiveness of any organized crime intelligence gathering activity can be greatly increased by the use of electronic surveillance and wiretapping because of the nature of most organized crime business discussions, which take place for the most part over the telephone or in face-to-face secured meeting places. In those states where the utilization of wiretapping or electronic surveillance as defined by Title III (see Chapter 9) is prohibited, agents are limited to normal surveillance activities or the use of electronic recording equipment in conjunction with informers or undercover agents engaged in consensual conversations with organized crime suspects.

In jurisdictions where court authorization can be obtained for electronic eavesdropping and wiretap surveillance activities, recording equipment is used to pick up targeted conversations and then preserved for later possible use. Often transcripts are prepared of such discussions for entry into the intelligence system. Specially trained agents are used in achieving the court authorized wiretap or electronic surveillance.

The importance of such surveillance in organized crime intelligence operations as well as for prosecutions cannot be deemphasized. Although conversations between organized crime members are often coded by various methods to disguise identity and subject

---

[11]*Id.* at p. 4–6.

matter, astute analysts and agents can usually break the codes and identify the speakers, the identities of persons discussed, and the subject matter at hand. Often information acquired by such means can lead to proof of associations between suspects and evidence acquired against top organized crime leaders.

Informers

The use of informers has been widespread in law enforcement for many years. Law enforcement officers frequently say that "an officer is only as good as his informers."[12] Informers provide a wide variety of needed information and are selected from diverse backgrounds. The selection, use and management of informants is often a difficult task. Efforts to recruit and select informants must be carefully considered before utilization of those informants.

Many persons use the terms "informer" or "informant" as synonymous with undercover agent. This clearly is not correct. An undercover agent is an experienced, highly trained, and motivated law enforcement officer who assumes a new underworld identity to infiltrate an organized crime group, often for long periods of time. The agent at the conclusion of his infiltration frequently becomes a chief witness in any subsequent criminal prosecution.

An informant, on the other hand, is not a law enforcement officer. Such a person generally takes a much more passive role than an undercover agent. Informants are used to obtain information and to assist law enforcement officers in targeting groups or individuals for further investigation or for the purposes of gaining an introduction of an undercover agent into a particular crime group. An informant's confidentiality is closely guarded, and he rarely if ever would appear in open court for the prosecution.

The informant's duties then include observation and collection of information, introduction of agents into organized crime groups, and selection of targeted individuals or groups for investigation. The informant's activities do not normally exceed these limited roles. The agent's duties would include acting upon the information provided by the informant and utilizing the contacts and

---

[12]E. D. Godfrey, et al., *supra*, note 8 at 20.

introductions of the informant so that further investigation and organized crime prosecution could take place.[13]

Informants often conjure up rather sleezy, degrading images; however, such persons are really as diverse as the society and so, too, are their motivations. The normal degrading image, while frequently true, is a gross overgeneralization. Sometimes, for example, respected ordinary citizens acting out of a sense of duty offer to provide information in this capacity.[14]

Informants can be categorized to certain degrees:

1. Felons,
2. Misdemeanants,
3. Persons arrested, awaiting trial, or sentencing,
4. Professional informants (those who earn their livelihood by this employment);
5. Honest or good citizens; and
6. Insiders.

Members of each group may have a variety of motivations for offering their specialized services to law enforcement. Not only must law enforcement officers be aware of their backgrounds but the various motivations of such individuals must also be considered. Such persons' motivations usually fall into one or more of the following:

1. *Duty:* Ordinary people who act out of a sense of duty or patriotism (rare but possible).

2. *Revenge:* People who act out of a sense of hate, i.e., "to get even."

3. *Favors:* Those who offer services as a bargaining tool (particularly as to those arrested or awaiting trial or sentencing).

4. *Fear:* Those who need police protection (typically insiders who have fallen out of good graces).

5. *Profit:* Those who provide information for a living, i.e., professional informants.

---

[13]See Herbert & Sinclair, "The Use of Minors as Undercover Agents or Informants: Some Legal Problems," 5, *The Journal of Police Science and Administration* (June, 1977).

[14]See, e.q., "The Car Dealer Who Nailed Joe Bonanno," *Newsweek*, p. 48 (October 13, 1980).

6. *Repentors:*	Those who wish for one reason or another to start fresh and make up for past wrongs (this too is rare, but it does occur from time to time).
7. *Crackpots:*	Those whose motivations are distorted by reason of certain psychological or psychiatric problems (this is a common occurrence, and there are many such individuals especially in large metropolitan areas).
8. *Egotists:*	Those who wish to make a name for themselves.
9. *Confidence Men:*	Those who seek money for false information.[15]

Often, potential informants contact law enforcement officers and offer assistance. This is done for a variety of reasons and motivations. Although such persons must be cautiously handled, much more care must be exercised by law enforcement officers in the handling of persons who have been arrested or those awaiting trial and sentencing. While cooperation can often be very beneficial to all involved in such circumstances, negotiations by law enforcement without such an informant's counsel may very well interfere with the informant's Sixth Amendment right to counsel. Moreover, such negotiations could result in defense attacks upon the whole process as attempts to secure confessions through improper means (thereby negating any consent given to a statement procured by such an alleged fraud or misrepresentation) or as plea-bargaining, often enforceable through the courts or perhaps even contempt of court if the officer interferes with the judicial or sentencing process. As a consequence, great care as to these potential informants must be followed. The informant's counsel must become involved early in the discussions, and a proper waiver of constitutional rights obtained. Moreover, confidential acknowledgements should be obtained from the informant and his counsel to clearly indicate the discussions and to maintain a proper record.

Prior to beginning any utilization of an informant, a personal interview must be conducted and certain basic information must

---

[15]Ohio, *supra,* note 9, Confidential Sources Section.

be obtained. After the personal interview, the assessment of the informant's identity category and motivations, and the screening out of those persons readily excludable (crackpots), certain practical judgments must be made. First, there must be a realistic assessment of the potential informers proximity to principals of illegal activities. Second, there must be consideration of the informant's contacts and other logical connections to organized crime targets. Third, there must be an evaluation of the informant's motivations and the possible conflicts of interest that those motivations could create with valid law enforcement objectives. If a determination is made that the informant can be effectively utilized, because he is close to targeted groups and activities and can be controlled despite his motivations, he should then be selected.

After selection, the identity of the informer must be closely guarded. That identity should be known to the recruiting officer and the head of the intelligence unit only. A secure file containing the informant's confidential information and history should be kept but coded only by number. His record should be periodically monitored and information obtained from him should be put into that record so that he can be properly and effectively evaluated as time goes on. Moreover, that provides a basis upon which conclusions can be made as to an informant's reliability, which is often of special significance in the acquisition of search and eavesdropping warrants (see Chapter 14).

So long as the informants do not become involved in specific criminal activity nor witness such activity, law enforcement officers may generally claim that such informant's identity is confidential and not subject to disclosure (see *Rovario u United States*, 353 U.S. 53, 1957).

In some cases, informants must be paid to obtain information or to sustain them through the period of cooperation. "Justice Funds" or the like are frequently used for cash payments to such persons, although the controlling officer is usually required to sign for the release of such funds under oath swearing as to its use and purposes, with the concurrance and approval of his superior.

Proper selection, management, and use of informants can lead to the provision of very valuable law enforcement information. Improper selection, negligent management, or poor direction can lead to a variety of problems including risk to the informant and the agent, criminal activity by the informant, and embarrassment to the agency. Informants must be strictly conditioned as to their activities, and if problems arise they should be pulled out of the program. What they can and cannot do must be spelled out, and an acknowledgement as to those conditions must be secured.

Undercover Operations

Successful clandestine undercover law enforcement infiltration of organized crime groups is quite difficult. Often, to be successful, such operations must continue for many months or even years. In addition, the selected agent or agents must be highly trained and motivated, money for the operation must be available, many sacrifices must be made, and many risks must be taken by the individual agent. The usual culmination of undercover efforts results in prosecution with the agent often being the main witness.

Initially, for such operations, a targeted group is selected by the use of intelligence information already contained within the intelligence system. Analysis of the information is used to match an agent by personality, ethnic traits, background, and other socioeconomic factors so that he may be placed within the group and readily blend within such group. A cover story, necessary documents, living quarters, and a whole new life-style must be arranged, following which the agent will be placed within the community. Often, an introduction into the group is made through the use of informants.

Regular contact through "safe" checkpoints and meeting places must be maintained to ensure agent safety. A careful log of day-to-day actions and activities must be kept by the agent for input of information and later recall and use if necessary. Drop-points for such written or recorded information must be selected by prior arrangement and care must be exercised to maintain the cover and to make sure the drop-points and meeting places are not discovered. Undercover operations must be subject to certain requirements and safeguards.

Often undercover agents and informants can provide a wealth of very specific information to intelligence units. When engaged in securing evidential intelligence information, such agents or informants can often, through body recorders, obtain good evidence of criminal conversations, conspiracy as to planned criminal activities, as well as a host of other incriminating conversations. The proper use of such devices neither is subject to the requirements of the federal Title III Electronic Surveillance Statute nor does it violate any constitutional prohibition (see *On Lee v United States*, 343 U.S. 747, 1952). (See also *United States v White*, 401 U.S. 745, 1971; *Hoffa v United States*, 385 U.S. 293, 1966; *Lopez v United States*, 373 U.S. 427, 1963.)

Often, claims of entrapment will follow successful undercover operations that result in prosecution and trial. Entrapment, an affirmative defense to a crime charge, can be defined as government creation and encouragement of criminal activity by a person otherwise indisposed to commit that activity, so as to make the criminal conduct the product of law enforcement activity, rather than an outgrowth of the criminal predisposition of the subject. It does not, however, include the governments' affording of mere opportunities or facilities for the commission of offenses. "[E]ntrapment is the *manufacturing* of crime by law enforcement officials and their agents."[16] A more complete examination of the defense may be obtained through an examination of two major United States Supreme Court cases: *Sorrells v United States*, 287 U.S. 435 (1932); and *Sherman v United States*, 356 U.S. 369 (1958).

The strong differences of opinion among the Justices deciding these cases highlight the two manners in which the defense of entrapment can be explained: (1) an examination of the predisposition of the defendant to commit the crime, or (2) an examination of law enforcement conduct in inducing or assisting the commission of the crime. Although the majority opinions espoused the first of these potential views, it is also clear that the more outrageous and unconscionable the police conduct, the more likely the court may be to find the existence of entrapment as a matter of law.

Regardless of the differences between the two views, the law, as formulated by the majority decision in both *Sorrells* and *Sherman*, focuses inquiry on the defendant's predisposition to commit criminal activity. If he or she is so predisposed (as determined

---

[16]*Lopez v United States*, 373 U.S. 427, 434 (1963).

essentially by the facts) and if the government merely provides the means or facilities to be used in the commission of crime, entrapment claims will not be successful. Entrapment cannot be successfully claimed if the government in the course of under-cover operations "traps" a suspect in the course of those operations. So long as that person possessed the necessary predisposition to commit the activity, the defense, although subject to assertion, will not comport to the legal requirements for successful utilization.

The use of undercover operations in conjunction with the other covert intelligence collection activities is on the increase. Recently, successful efforts have been put forth by the FBI to achieve very deep and very high infiltration of organized crime groups. These efforts have resulted in successful information acquisitions as well as prosecutions of top organized crime leaders.

Often, in the course of undercover operations some rather difficult choices must be made. For example, should an agent use alcohol or drugs, should he or she have sexual relations with targeted subjects in the course of maintaining their cover, should he or she be involved in criminal activity and, if so, to what extent, should he or she warn of impending "hits" or stop them? The answers to these questions may vary from operation to operation, but generally the agent must always stop short of committing serious crime or allowing such crime to take place.[17]

EVALUATION

Once information is collected and put into the system, a two-fold reliability assessment must be made to encode that information. The first such encoding is that used to determine whether or not the information is in all likelihood *factually true*, while the second test centers on assessing the *truthfulness* and *reliability* of the *source* of the information. Often, scales are used for this purpose placing a numerical valuation of 1–5 or 1–10 for such facts.

Evaluation and assessment of the factuality and reliability of information and its source is essential to the quality of the intelligence system. Improper grading of information is a waste of

---

[17]See Herbert, *supra*, Note 13.

time and money and endangers the whole operation including informants, agents, and the system's reports.

In order to properly carry on the evaluation function for information collected and subject to storage within the intelligence system, accurate source records must be maintained. This is particularly true as to material derived from informants. In addition, accurate historical information must be maintained so as to allow proper evaluation of the informant supplied material. Over time, assuming proper records are maintained, this reliability history can quite readily be traced and used for evaluation purposes.

Aside from the critical evaluative functions performed upon information and sources of that information put into the intelligence system, a thorough evaluation process can assist in case preparation functions as well (see Chapter 14). Often, for example, such information, in order to meet certain minimum constitutional safeguards, must be supplied to magistrates making determinations as to the existence of probable cause for the issuance of search warrants. In the course of these proceedings reliability assessments are critical for determination of both the factual basis for the information as well as its source reliability.

The collection and evaluation of information for an intelligence system is a significant and obviously necessary prerequisite to further information analysis and reporting. It is also the first real step ultimately leading to the development of strategies to deal with the problem of organized crime.

Chapter 12

COLLATION AND ANALYSIS OF INFORMATION

Once intelligence information is gathered and rated for factual validity and reliability of source in the evaluation process, the information must then be translated into intelligence. *Collation* of the raw information previously collected is really the first step in this translation process. Collation may be defined as the systematic storage of useful and relevant information in an orderly fashion, subject to quick retrieval, and arranged so that relationships between seemingly disconnected elements may be established through later analysis.[1]

Information storage is at the essence of the collation process. Storage, of course, can be physically accomplished through the utilization of filing or storage cabinets or it can be electronically achieved through the use of computer bases. Regardless of which method is used in any given intelligence system, information obtained through the collection process must be logically categorized and broken down by at least activities or subject matter, names, places, and businesses or organizations. Thus, for example, an intelligence report that indicated the following information should be stored under the following categories:

Report: John Jones and Louis Smith, an employee of XYZ Import Co., were observed together on August 8, 1980, at the Odysey Tavern. During this meeting John Jones handed Smith what was believed to be a package containing cocaine. Smith handed Jones a package believed to contain United States currency.

Storage Categories:

---

[1]E. D. Godfrey, Jr., and D. Harris, *Basic Elements of Intelligence: A Manual of Theory, Structure and Procedures For Use by Law Enforcement Agencies Against Organized Crime*, pp. 22–3 (Washington D.C., 1971).

> *Names:* John Jones and Louis Smith
> *Places:* Odysey Tavern
> *Activity:* Drugs (cocaine)
> *Businesses:* XYZ Import Co.; Odysey Tavern

In order for such information to be successfully utilized, it must be accurately cross-referenced so that a complete picture of any activities can be later obtained. Without cross-referencing, valuable information would be otherwise lost and impossible to accurately retrieve and analyze.

The indexing and cross-referencing process must be consistently followed if the system is to work properly. Uniformity of indexing and cross-referencing in the process is critical to the maintenance of an optimum system. Inconsistencies in subject matter inclusion or even the cross-referencing process can turn an otherwise excellent system into a quagmire of useless information beyond any effective analysis.

The advent of relatively low cost computer storage and retrieval information systems has greatly increased law enforcement's usage of such systems. Information can now be quickly stored and recalled and a much broader cross-referencing system can be used with computerized program systems. Moreover, with proper programming, the analysis function can also be greatly enhanced with the computer performing a wide variety of often routine and otherwise tedious and time-consuming functions, e.g., statistical or financial analysis.

Along with the advent of the computer, however, came certain risks associated with the security of computer stored information. Access to computer stored information, especially in situations where computers are time-shared with other governmental agencies, is a definite risk to such systems. However, with exclusive agency use and certain entrance coding precautions for informational access to the computer, the risks can be minimized although not entirely eliminated.

Once the collation process has been completed, information must undergo analysis to convert that information into useful and significant intelligence. It has been said that analysis is the very heart of an intelligence system inasmuch as the function "assembles the bits and pieces of information that have been collected . . . and puts them together in such a manner as to show pattern and meaning."[2]

The task of information conversion falls upon the shoulders of the analysts. "Analysts, utilizing information supplied by investigators, make judgmental decisions concerning the short- and long-term implications of criminal activity in terms of tactical operations and strategic assessment. . . . The analyst looks beyond specific cases to ascertain the similarities and differences among many different cases."[3]

Generally, the pure analysis function involves the development of a hypothesis based upon the information previously provided to the analyst through the collection and evaluation function. A hypothesis might be defined as a working theory or unproven supposition, tentatively used to explain certain facts and provide a basis for further investigative efforts designed to establish the existence or nonexistence of the proposition. Some have defined an intelligence hypothesis as a conjectural statement about the relationships that exist among two or more given variables.[4] Others have defined a hypothesis in an intelligence setting as a tool the analyst uses "to develop a tentative explanation for some criminal activity."[5]

Once the hypothesis is formed by the analyst upon the basis of the previously collected information as analyzed, the hypothesis must be tested to determine its own validity and, if necessary, reformulated or adjusted as required. The testing procedure is first conducted with information already at hand by the analyst from within the intelligence system. Usually, however, more information is necessary to fully test the hypothesis. Often, the analyst may find it necessary to develop several different alternative hypotheses, or further information acquisition would be limited.

In the course of testing any hypothesis, the analyst must consequently request the collection of more information by the unit investigator or other law enforcement agent. Generally the collector will be given a series of specific requests for information by the analyst and a series of individual or group targets to monitor, most

---

[2]*Id* at 24.

[3]D. Harris, Basic Elements of Intelligence: A Manual for Police Department Intelligence Units, p. 27 (Washington D.C. 1976 rev. ed.).

[4]See *Id* at 34.

[5]*Id* at 34

of whom the analyst would have previously selected through the targeting process heretofore discussed. The analyst's function is thus an ongoing process—a cyclic effort[6] that never really terminates. Information subjected to analysis, leading to the development of a hypothesis, generates the need for the acquisition of more information to test the hypothesis, which in turn is processed and provided to the analyst to confirm or disprove the hypothesis; most frequently, the hypothesis is adjusted with the new information and then retested. Consequently, the process really is circuitous and fact seeking as well as fact generating.

The hypothesis developed by the analyst is achieved through inductive reasoning. Inductive reasoning may be defined as a logical process by which a general conclusion (the hypothesis) is ultimately reached through progression from particular facts or individual cases to other facts or cases. It is to be distinguished from deductive reasoning, which may be defined as a logical reasoning process by which an ultimate fact or conclusion is deduced or derived from a number of existing facts.

The intelligence hypothesis development and testing process might be graphically depicted as shown in Figure 6.

It is important to note the ongoing circuitous process of the information flow within the system. In effect, the system never stops generating facts while at the same time demanding more facts.

Once such a hypothesis is developed, it might be tested to establish its own validity. Thus, new investigative efforts to acquire more specific information must be undertaken. These might include law enforcement undercover operations to infiltrate A.B.C. Contracting Company; wiretaps of Mr. Smith's, Mr. A's, and A.B.C.'s Contracting Company's phones; surveillance of the principals; and a variety of other efforts. Once enough information has been obtained to establish the hypothesis or to disprove the hypothesis, the appropriate enforcement response can be selected and, if indicated, followed.

Often the development, testing, and resultant validation of a hypothesis leads to clear indications of new organized crime trends, activities, or developments, i.e., strategic intelligence. Such indicators can be used to develop long-range enforcement responses and

---

[6]Delaware Department of Public Safety, Division of State Police, *Intelligence Central Standard Operating Procedures*, p. II-5.

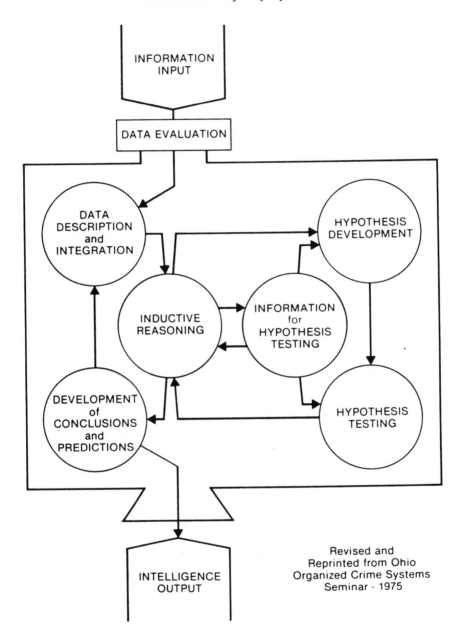

Figure 6. Hypothesis development and testing process.

strategies to counteract the predicted trends and activities. In addition, such validation actions frequently result in individual prosecutions of particular individuals or groups participating in organized crime activities. In either case however, the analysis function of hypothesis development and testing is an important and necessary law enforcement tool in any effective response to organized crime activities.

These are the steps in the development of a hypothesis and its testing:

1. Summarize relevant and available information.
2. Upon the basis of the information at hand develop an initial hypothesis.
3. Test the hypothesis with information from the intelligence unit.
4. Adjust the hypothesis with the use of internally derived information.
5. Test the selected information categories for information acquisition.
6. Request needed information from outside the system through targeting processes.
7. Receive and collate information derived from outside the intelligence system.
8. Test the hypothesis with externally derived information.
9. Adjust the hypothesis as necessary and repeat if necessary steps 3–8.
10. Derive the final hypothesis or conclusion and disseminate an intelligence report.

Aside from the development and testing of a working hypothesis, an intelligence analyst has several other valuable and extremely important functions if the organized crime intelligence process is to be totally effective. In the course of performing those functions, the analyst must perform a wide variety of research activities and utilize a multitude of research tools to help in the intelligence analysis function. An examination of several of these will be important to an overall understanding of the analysis function within the complete intelligence system.

RESEARCH

An analyst must conduct various forms of general as well as specific research in order to properly perform his analysis function. For example, within the general research category, information from public sources about a wide variety of reported organized crime trends and activities must be obtained, researched, and analyzed principally as background information for the intelligence system. Moreover, in many cases, specific research activities must be conducted to bolster particular investigations. This task generally falls upon the shoulders of the analyst, who is usually trained by education and experience to carry out these functions.

The research findings and information so derived often assists in not only providing a foundation for the intelligence information base but also for the initial hypothesis development.

Aside from research activities to develop an informational base for the intelligence system and for specific case needs, research must often be conducted to fill information gaps or voids, to develop plans for other collection efforts, to respond to particular informational requests, and to produce intelligence reports. Research can be conducted in a wide variety of ways and from a number of sources, many of which we discussed in the preceding chapter.

TACTICAL INTELLIGENCE REQUEST RESPONSES

Often, an intelligence analyst will be asked to provide specific information to support ongoing criminal investigations. Generally, the necessary responses to such requests must be supported with background information to give the enforcement unit an overall and complete response. This is an important and valuable function of the analyst.

ANALYSIS FUNCTIONS

One of the most important functions of the analysis process is the utilization of various techniques to assist the overall intelligence effort and in many cases to help formulate or test either a strategic or tactical intelligence hypothesis. Moreover, these techniques can greatly assist in the targeting process, the allocation of resources and manpower to particular areas of concern, and in some cases can be used in prosecutorial efforts against particular persons or groups. Important techniques to the organized crime intelligence process might be categorized as follows:

1. Targeting Analysis.
2. Financial Analysis.
3. Statistical Data Analysis.
4. Flow Charting/Time-sequence Analysis.
5. Association Matrix/Link-Network Diagraming Analysis.

Targeting Analysis

As we have previously mentioned, the targeting process is a function of the intelligence system by which the focus of investigative efforts is narrowed to very particular areas, groups, or persons. Such efforts are designed to hone in on a given target for a more intensive examination, often with prosecutorial objectives in mind. Targeting is a necessary analyst function that helps conserve agency funds and resources and assists in allocation of those resources to the most beneficial and potentially successful area.

Financial Analysis

A number of financial analysis techniques can quite readily be adapted for specific purposes to organized crime investigations. Often, for example, it becomes important for an analyst to determine an individual's source of cash flow or income to determine probable illegitimate profits derived from illegal activities. Other times it may be important to use different techniques to establish income based upon an asset accumulation theory. Frequently, such information can give valuable clues to profits derived from specific organized crime activities or groups.

There are two main methods of estimating income derived from nonapparent or illegal sources: (1) *Cash Flow Analysis* (including *expenditure methods*, to determine if expenditures exceed income, and *deposits methods*, to determine if deposits exceed income) and (2) *Net Worth Analysis*. An examination of each technique should assist in the overall understanding of the analysis function.

CASH FLOW ANALYSIS. Cash flow analysis involves the examination and comparison of an individual's or group's income (often through an examination of deposits) with that person's or group's expenditures. If a targeted person's known or earned legitimate income, for example, exceeds his apparent or known expenditures, then that person apparently is living within his means and perhaps saving money as well. So long as his savings (which are sometimes unknown) do not amass at a greater or faster rate than his apparent legitimate income after deduction of expenditures then a likely conclusion to derive from that analysis would be that he has no source of illegitimate income.

If an examination of another person's cash flow reveals expenditures at or slightly above income from legitimate sources, the same conclusions would probably be in order. However, if expenditures are greatly exceeding known legitimate income sources or deposits, that person or entity would be a likely subject for further investigation inasmuch as it would appear that he or it would have more to spend (possibly derived from illicit sources) than he or it should have at hand.

Generally, cash flow analysis takes place after the targeting process has focused information collection activities upon a given individual or group. Frequently, surveillance activities, public records searches, informants, and other covert information collection activities or sources will reveal a consistent pattern of income expenditures. Even when exact expenditure information is not available, costs can usually be estimated with some accuracy. Once all of these costs or expenditures are compared with legitimate or known income sources, a fairly accurate estimate of (potential) illegally derived income can be made and utilized by the analyst.

NET WORTH ANALYSIS. Like cash flow analysis, net worth analysis can be used to make fairly accurate estimates of what may amount to illegally derived income. Any individual's net worth is derived by adding up his or her total assets (all of that person's valuable possessions) and liabilities (all of that person's debts) and subtracting those liabilities from those assets. The end result is the individual's net worth (the amount by which his assets exceed his liabilities). While some individuals have no net worth due to poverty and others may have negative net worths (and are therefore bankrupt), most people have some net worth. Changes in the net worth vary from year to year and may go up or down depending upon the individual's financial successes or failures during the year. The variations or changes in net worth from year to year may be examined to determine an individual's illegally derived income.

The use of these financial data analysis tools are becoming much more commonplace in organized crime intelligence operations. They have been used for years by, among others, the Internal Revenue Service to tax previously unreported income. They are simple, practical, and highly effective analysis tools. In the real world, the use of such tools becomes slightly more complicated due to inflation, increase of property valuations, depreciation of certain goods, payment of interest, or repayment of personal loans. Despite such problems, these techniques have considerable practical value.

Statistical Data Analysis

Although probabilities and statistical analysis can be quite complicated as well as beyond the real scope of this text, several important matters must be briefly discussed. Statistical quantification, or the assignment of numerical valuations to particular verbalized assessments of information, is commonplace in the intelligence process. Such assessments must be made in the evaluation function for information as we discussed in the preceding chapter as well as in the analysis information function. Reliability assessment, for example, for the factual input of the intelligence system must be made if proper analysis is to be performed upon those facts. Such quantification assessment of both source reliability and factual basis for information is a necessary evaluation step (see Chapter 11).

Statistical techniques can also be used to compute percentages for financial analysis, to reach averages (mean, mode and median) for making income projections and evaluations, and for certain deductive reasoning tasks. They are helpful in the entire analysis process.

Flow Charting/Time Sequence Analysis

Sometimes in the analysis process, the mass of information to be analyzed becomes unmanageable unless put in proper sequence. A relatively simple way to make that information manageable is by the use of flow charting techniques. These visual aids simply allow the pictorial display of events or procedures in an orderly fashion for ease of examination and analysis. A simple flow chart depicting events or procedures from beginning to end would look something like that depicted in Figure 7.

Important events can be interspersed in the circles or squares between time element lines to show the events in proper time flow. Quite complex sequential events can thus be charted and followed with ease. If, for example, there are a number of sequential steps happening all at once, within one or more time sequences, a "critical path" can be added to the flow chart along with all other sequential events to allow complete analysis (see Figure 7).

Time/Series charts can also be used to pictorially graph relevant quantities of actions in given time periods. This technique is used to pictorially report, for example, burglaries, murders, robberies, and the similar instances in many cities' annual crime reports. The graphic presentation is depicted as shown in Figure 8.

By using such methods, increases or decreases in given actions may be charted, and by continuing on the line of demonstrated and proven occurrences, projections might be made as to future occurrences.

With the aid of similar graphs, predictions of the probable number of cargo thefts in the next month or for that matter for the remainder of the year can be made. Resources can then be allocated along with manpower for enforcement efforts.

In the eventuality that the graph is not a straight line (almost always), a midpoint line graph should be used so as to place an equal number of dotted activities in given months above and below the projection line (which would be a "mean"

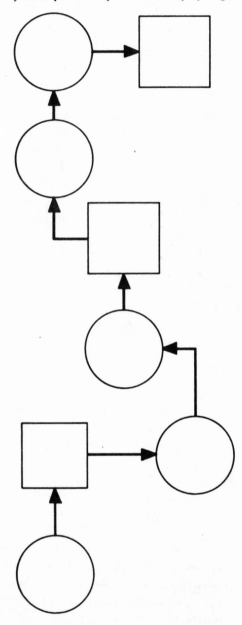

Reprinted from the Ohio Organized
Crime System One - 1975 Seminar

Figure 7. Event flow chart.

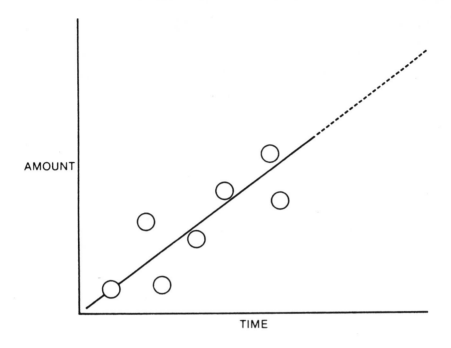

Major steps required are:
1. Lay out an appropriate scale on both axes
2. Plot existing data points using both axes
3. Label each axis
4. By visual estimation — draw a line close to the
   center of the data points
5. Extend the line for a trend estimate into
   the future

Reprinted from Ohio Organized
Crime System One Seminar - 1975

Figure 8. Time-series projection chart.

averaging projection, with half of the event dots above and half
below).

Association Matrix/Link Network Diagraming Analysis

Perhaps the most useful tool in the arsenal of analysis techniques for organized crime investigations is the Association Matrix/
Link Network Diagram Analysis. This technique may be defined

as an analytical tool used for the graphic representation of associations between persons and organizations.[7]

In the past, link network analysis techniques have been used by a variety of professions to help solve a myriad of practical problems, including production equipment layout systems, communication and control systems, and most recently law enforcement investigative systems. The analysis technique has most recently been applied by law enforcement intelligence operations in an effort to help uncover complex organized crime groups.[8]

The link network analysis technique is very useful in establishing probable organizational structures for organized crime individuals, groups, businesses, and organizations, in selecting probable leaders and often middle management personnel for such structures, in targeting particular individuals or businesses for further investigation, and in pictorially depicting organized crime organizations and associations. The process is composed of six separate steps:

1. Assembly of information.
2. Abstract of relative information as to individuals and affiliations.
3. Development of an association matrix.
4. Development of a preliminary link diagram.
5. Incorporation of organizational overlays into the diagram.
6. Refine the diagram.[9]

The link network analysis technique was applied to law enforcement use to assist in "systematically establish[ing] the relationship that exists among individuals and organizations from [a wide variety of] bits and pieces of available evidence."[10] Moreover, "it is systematic in its application; and it produces an easily assimilated, graphic portrayal of complex relationships."[11]

The process of link network analysis focuses on the recognition

---

[7]From Harper, W. R. & Harris, D. H. "The Applications of Link Analysis to Police Intelligence," *The Human Factors Society, Inc.* 17:2, pp. 157–164, 1975.

[8]*Id.*

[9]*Id.*

[10]*Id.*

[11]*Id.*

and determination of the presence or absence of connections or links between persons and various organizations or activities. The strength of the probable association must be rated through at least three rating categories: (1) *strong connections* (strong links), (2) *weak connections* (weak links), and (3) *no connections* (no links). A more sophisticated rating system would add a fourth rating choice: (4) *moderate connections* (moderate links).

Once the available information has been assembled from the intelligence system and abstracted as to individuals and affiliations, an association matrix is developed to record the evaluated associations. The matrix is composed of an isosceles triangle, with one 90° angle at its base and two 45° angles at its ends. The triangle is divided into square cells with an equal number of horizontal and vertical axis squares. The number of squares along each axis is selected by determination of the number of individuals to be analyzed for associations. The individuals are then arranged alphabetically and listed along the horizontal plane left to right alphabetically and along the vertical plane top to bottom alphabetically. The matrix for use in the examination of associations between five persons might look like Figure 9.

If, for example, six persons, named Mr. Alpha, Mr. Beta, Mr. Gamma, Mr. Delta, Mr. Epsilon, and Mr. Zeta, are to be analyzed for associations based upon intelligence data, the matrix would look like Figure 10.

From the available information, an evaluative analysis of the strength of associations between these six individuals is made and then graphically depicted within each cell where the cells converge between the names along the horizontal and vertical planes. Utilizing a four-strength "dot" evaluation method (= strong association or link; = moderate association or link; 0 = weak association or link; no entry for no association or link), suppose a strong association between Alpha and Beta, a moderate association between Delta and Zeta, a weak association between Alpha and Delta, a strong association between Alpha and Epsilon, and no association between Zeta and Alpha, the matrix would look like Figure 11.

Once this evaluative step is completed and placed within the matrix cells, the number of cell associations is counted and placed below the horizontal plane below each individual's name, as depicted

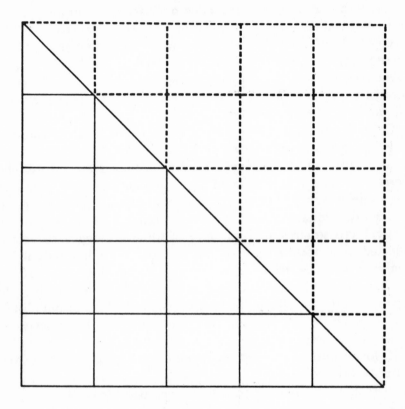

Reprinted from Ohio Organized
Crime System One Seminar · 1975

Figure 9. Association matrix.

in Figure 11. In order to count the associations, the horizontal and vertical axis cells must be counted where a link appears.

Once the matrix is completed and the associations counted, the next step of the procedure uses the graphic development of a link network diagram. In the diagramming process, different pictorial devices are used to demonstrate persons and associations, the strength of those associations, and organizational overlays once the diagram is initially completed.

Persons are depicted in the diagram with circles, organizations with boxes, and associations with lines. Strong associations or

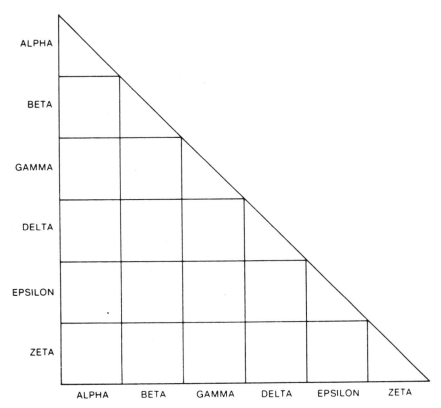

Figure 10. Association matrix example.

links are depicted as solid lines, moderate associations or links
with broken lines, weak associations or links with dotted lines, and
no association with no lines:

Strong Association Links: ─────────────────────────

Moderate Association Links: ─ ─ ─ ─ ─ ─ ─ ─ ─ ─ ─ ─ ─

Weak Association Links: . . . .

No Association Links:

Normally the graphic diagram should begin with the placement of the individual with the most links in the center of the
page and then proceeding to add individuals to the diagram in the
order of most associations to the least associations. Although the
preliminary graph might have crossed or bent association lines,

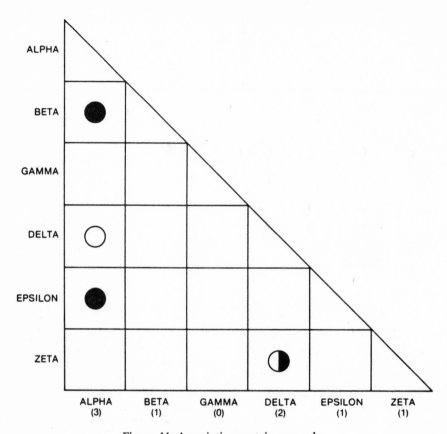

Figure 11. Association matrix example.

no association lines should ultimately cross or deviate from a straight line from person to person. In the course of refining the graph, individuals can be moved throughout the graphic presentation until straight link lines between each individual can be achieved. In the example given above, the graph for the associations would be depicted as follows in Figure 12.

The number of connections between any given circularly depicted person and another so depicted person must equal the number of connections or links as fixed along the horizontal axis of the association matrix. Once the diagram is first drawn it may have to be adjusted several times until no lines cross or bend. After that is

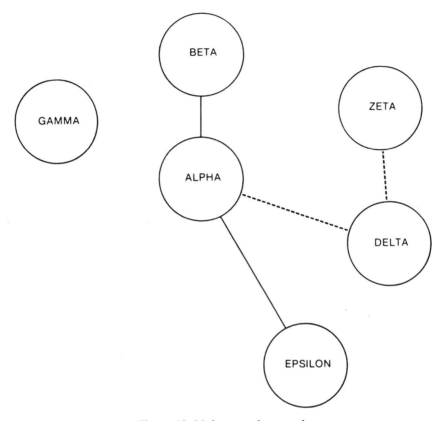

Figure 12. Link network example.

completed, organizational overlays should be utilized to show not only the relationships or associations between persons but also among and between those persons and organizations. If, in our example, it is learned that Mr. Alpha and Mr. Beta operate the A.B. Motel, Inc., while Alpha and Epsilon are partners in the Sleezy Towel Supply Company, the overlays in the diagram would look like Figure 13.

Often, tentative conclusions (hypotheses) can be drawn readily from such link diagrams pinpointing probable leaders, middle management personnel, interrelationship of activities and organizations, and similar matters. When evaluating such considerations,

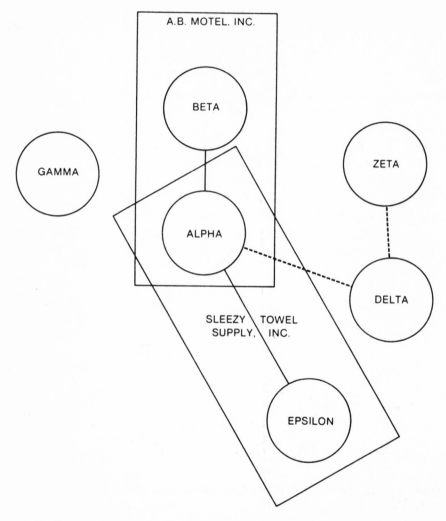

Figure 13. Link network example with organizational overlay.

it is important to keep in mind the insulating characteristics of most organized crime groups and not jump to the conclusion that the person with the most connections is the obvious leader. Depending upon the given facts in our example, the leader of this organization (assuming that is what it is) could be any one of the individuals except Mr. Gamma, who should be now deleted from the diagram. Based upon our knowledge of organized crime and its general insulating tendencies, the probable leader in the diagram would be Mr. Delta, with Mr. Zeta as his advisor and with Mr. Alpha as his middle management person. That conclusion would then be subject to verification through the hypothesis testing procedure. Aside from the use of the diagram for graphic depiction of organizations and associations between individuals, it can also assist in targeting individuals for further investigative activities.

The association matrix and link network diagram techniques are valuable intelligence tools extremely useful in organized crime investigations. They are also useful in obtaining information about an organization and in uncovering "the hierarchial structure within a criminal organization or the interlocking structure of a combination of legitimate and illegitimate organizations."[12] The technique is of great value in depicting large and complex organizations. To demonstrate the usefulness of this technique within a large group of thirteen persons, having ninety-one possible associations and an overlap of four businesses, consider the following association matrix and link diagram using a three strength association link system (see Figures 14 and 15).

Increasingly, the analysis function, including the development of link network association matrixes and diagrams, is being conducted through computer analysis. The ease with which these systems perform such functions can only foretell of ever-increasing computer use. All segments of our society are affected by the advent of the computer, which has become an obsession with many. The 1980s, for example, have been characterized as "The Computer Age." The increased utilization of computer programming within intelligence units cannot be underestimated. There appears to be no question that once the intelligence process is completely integrated into a fully computerized system it will become much more efficient and effective. Moreover, the computer will be able to handle a much larger flow of information than can be done by hand. Information storage can thus be greatly enhanced. Perhaps the most effective utilization of the computer will come through extremely fast information retrieval as well as

---

[12]*Id* at 158.

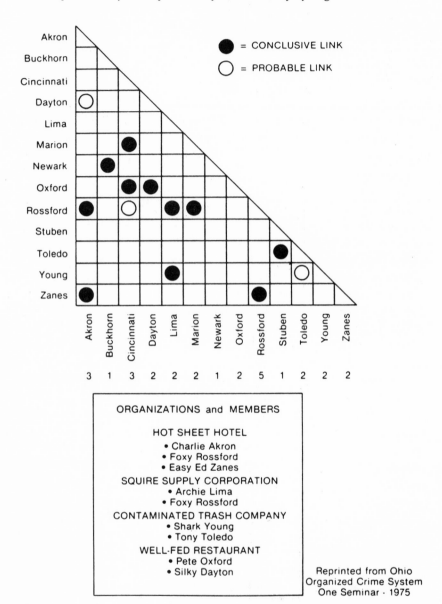

Figure 14. Association matrix example.

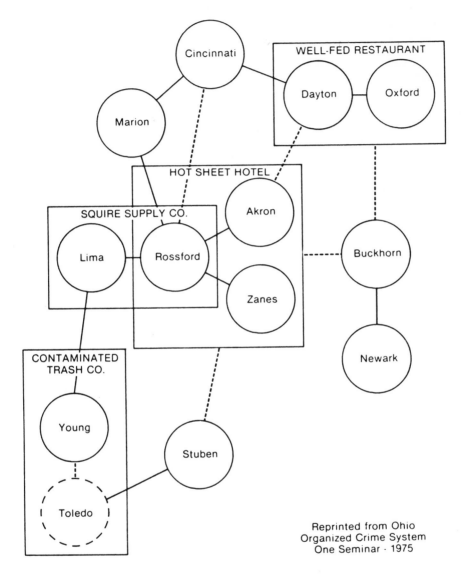

Figure 15. Link diagram example with organizational overlay.

built-in collation systems and analysis techniques.

Aside from the storage and retrieval advantages inherent in any computerized intelligence system, the analyst's function will be greatly enhanced through the use of computer programming. The computer will be able to do basic associations and correlations that any analyst would spend many hours, if not many days, doing. In many cases, the computer should be able to help in obtaining much more accurate projections for given organized crime activities and should greatly assist in the allocation of resources and manpower to counteract and overcome those predictions and projections. Moreover, the computer can be used to provide information to counteract organized crime activities before they take place and assist greatly in the development of prospective enforcement measures.

Although many analysis techniques (including the use of link analysis and computer storage and analysis modes for intelligence information) have been strenuously criticized by some, the increased utilization of these methods will surely continue. Allegations, for example, that link analysis amounts to "guilt by association"[13] are really misplaced. The technique is used to develop indications of association for hypothesis development and testing. Even if an evidentiary intelligence function is underway, the best the technique can hope to accomplish at the pre-indictment stage is the development of probable cause, which is certainly something less than the standard of proof required for the establishment of guilt. Moreover, the technique's real purpose lies in the development of strategic intelligence, in the targeting process, and in the development of a focus for further investigative efforts.

The collation and analysis functions of the intelligence system are critical components, surely the guts of the system. All enforcement and strategic efforts flow from these critical functions. Once these functions are completed, the system moves a notch to begin the dissemination and utilization of such information.

---

[13]Applegate, "The Business Papers Rule: Personal Privacy and White Collar Crime," *16 Akron Law Review*, pp. 189, 195–6 (Fall 1982).

Chapter 13

RETENTION, DISSEMINATION, AND
UTILIZATION OF INFORMATION

One of the most critical organized crime enforcement considerations and problems stems from the retention, dissemination,
and ultimate use of information developed by and as a result of an
intelligence system. In 1967 the President's Crime Commission in
it's *Report* found:

> Agencies do not cooperate with each other in preparing cases, and they do
> not exchange information with each other. Enforcement officers do not
> trust each other for they are sensitive to organized crimes ability to
> corrupt law enforcement. Agencies have not developed strategies to over-
> come these problems and to ensure that needed data can be effectively
> transferred.[1]

The Commission noted further:

> [L]aw enforcement agencies must share information and coordinate their
> plans.[2]
> [Interstate system should be created to] permit and encourage greater
> exchange of information . . . [3]

Ultimately, the Commission made two recommendations designed to encourage greater cooperation among police agencies
and increase exchange of information among those agencies:

> The federal government should create a central computerized office into
> which each Federal Agency would feed all of its organized crime intelligence.[4]
> The Department of Justice should give financial assistance to encourage
> the development of efficient systems for regional intelligence gathering,

---

[1]The President's Commission on Law Enforcement and Administration of Justice,
The Challenge of Crime in a Free Society: A Report, p. 199 (Washington D.C., 1967).

[2]*Id* at 204.

[3]*Id* at 206.

[4]*Id* at 204.

175

collection and dissemination. By financial assistance and provisions of security clearance, the Department should also sponsor and encourage research by the many relevant disciplines regarding the nature, development, activities, and organization of these special crime groups.[5]

For a plethora of reasons, including those noted by the President's Commission, dissemination, retention, exchange, and ultimate utilization of organized crime intelligence data has been greatly hampered for many years. Often, as pointed out in previous chapters, enforcement officials are reluctant to exchange information. These are the most often quoted reasons for this failure:

1. Law enforcement fear of public official corruption and concomitant disclosure of information to organized crime figures.
2. Political jealousies existing between and among different jurisdictional law enforcement groups.
3. Insufficient training or expertise of certain recipient departments (i.e., "they wouldn't know what to do with the information if they had it").
4. Legal prohibitions limiting or hampering the exchange of information within or between jurisdictional levels.

While there has been some justification for the refusal of information to suspect or ill trained enforcement agencies, there can be no support for a failure to exchange information due to political jealousies existing between either political parties, governmental units, or enforcement agencies and similar offices. Moreover, the information inhibitions created by legal prohibitions arising from certain statutes and administrative regulations unnecessarily hamper the exchange of information even among agencies at the same governmental level, no less between agencies of different governmental levels.

In the aftermath of Watergate and with a mind's eye focused on the year 1984 and George Orwell's predictions made in his work by the same title, Congress and some state legislators have been directing their attention to "privacy legislation." For the most part, this legislation has been promulgated to protect individuals

---

[5]*Id.* at 206.

from the piercing eye of the government. The legislation in general has concentrated upon the following subject areas:

1. Regulation of the collection of information as to individuals;
2. Regulation and control as to the dissemination of that information;
3. Creation of individual rights of access to that information;
4. Creation of individual remedies to challenge alleged erroneous information;
5. Creation of a statutory right to privacy (i.e., "the right to be left alone").

Congress and the various state legislatures have been active in the privacy area, partly because of the fact that the United States Constitution does not absolutely create nor protect a constitutional right to privacy. The Constitution through the First, Fourth, Fifth, Ninth, and Fourteenth Amendments does provide some privacy protections, although an absolute right to privacy is not expressly provided for in that charter. Consequently, legislation is necessary if specific rights to privacy are to be protected.

Although Congress has no direct legislative authority in the area of privacy, the power to pass such legislation is generally founded upon the following:

1. Congress's right to regulate interstate commerce (see U.S. Constitution, Article I, Section 8, Clause 3).
2. Congress's right to oversee the spending of federal money.
3. Congress's right to provide regulations regarding the operation of the federal government.

Congress's power to regulate interstate commerce is one of the greatest and most frequently used constitutional powers that Congress evokes when enacting legislation. The spending power and the right to oversee the operation of certain aspects of the federal government (aside from the President's power to do so within the Executive Branch) is an awesome but indirect tool that Congress utilizes to influence some action over which it has no direct legislative control.

The federal government has been active in the privacy area since the 1970s, when it began to enact privacy legislation.

To date, the following significant privacy legislation has been enacted:

1. The Family Educational Rights and Privacy Act of 1974, Public Law 93-380, 88 Statute 571 (August 21, 1974), which is now codified in 20 U.S.C. §1232g. This Act controls the collection, retention, and dissemination of information kept by educational institutions only.
2. The Federal Privacy Act of 1974, Public Law 93-579, 88 Statute 1896 (January 1, 1975), now codified in 5 U.S.C. §552a.
3. The First Amendment Privacy Protection Act of 1980, Public Law 96-440, 94 Statute 1879 (Oct. 13, 1980), now codified in 42 U.S.C. §2000aa *et seq.* This Act covers the seizure of materials held by members of the media for publication.

The Federal Privacy Act generally prohibits the disclosure of personal information that is contained in a system of records kept by the federal government or any of its agencies unless a general or specific exemption applies allowing release of information. One of the exemptions allowing release of information applies to law enforcement requests for information. The Act's nondisclosure prohibitions do not apply as to information provided to law enforcement agencies. In this regard the Act provides:

> Information may be released "to another agency or to an instrumentality of any governmental jurisdiction within or under the control of the United States for a civil or criminal law enforcement activity if the activity is authorized by law, and if the head of the agency or instrumentality has made a written request to the agency which maintains the record specifying the particular portion desired and the law enforcement activity for which the record is sought."[6]

The Privacy Act also contains general as well as specific exemptions as to information to be supplied to law enforcement agencies. The Act, in addition, gives each federal agency the authority to promulgate rules in accordance with the provisions of the Act. Such rules have been promulgated by over thirty-five federal agencies including the C.I.A., the Department of Justice, and the Treasury Department. Moreover, certain agencies, including the

---

[6]See 5 U.S.C. §552(b)(7)(1974).

C.I.A. and federal agencies engaged in law enforcement activities, have general exemptions as to most criminal investigative material. In addition, certain specific exemptions contained in the Privacy Act allow certain agencies to refuse access to certain specified records. These include all noncriminal law enforcement activities designated as "investigatory." Also included is the right to withhold materials that would identify or name a confidential source if there has been an expressed promise to protect the identity of that source.

The Privacy Act provisions, as well as the individual agency rules promulgated pursuant to the Act, have limited or prevented altogether full information disclosure from federal agencies to other federal agencies or to state or local agencies. Moreover, confusing interpretations placed upon the Act and its provisions and the administrative regulations promulgated thereunder have also led to disclosure problems.

Other federal laws have also created disclosure problems to law enforcement agencies. The Freedom of Information Act, first enacted into law in 1966 and amended in 1967 and 1974 and now codified in 5 U.S.C. §552(b), provided the other side to the Privacy Act. This Act requires disclosure of certain federally collected and retained information upon request, unless the information sought is exempted from disclosure by other provisions of the Act. Certain law enforcement investigative materials are exempted from disclosure under the following provisions:

> [Information need not be disclosed if the information is] investigatory records compiled for law enforcement purposes, but only to the extent that the production of such records would (A) interfere with enforcement proceedings, (B) deprive a person of a right to a fair trial or an impartial adjudication, (C) constitute an unwarranted invasion of personal privacy, (D) disclose the identity of a confidential source and, in the case of a record compiled by a criminal law enforcement authority in the course of a criminal investigation, or by an agency conducting a lawful national security intelligence investigation, confidential information furnished only by the confidential source, (E) disclose investigative techniques and procedures, or (F) endanger the life or physical safety of law enforcement personnel.[7]

Whereas the Privacy Act prohibits disclosure unless an exemp-

---

[7]5 U.S.C. §552(b)(7)(1974).

tion applies, the Freedom of Information Act requires disclosure unless an exemption applies prohibiting that disclosure. As to local or even federal law enforcement requests for information from federal agencies, however, both of the Acts have hampered the dissemination and exchange of criminal investigative information among agencies.

Many states have also been active in this area passing legislation similar to the Privacy Act and the federal Freedom of Information Act (which at the state level are commonly called public records acts). The states' efforts, especially when coupled with the federal efforts, have created a quagmire and a mass of confusion as to the right to access, disclosure, and dissemination of information to any law enforcement agency, even regarding organized crime activities.

In 1975, a federal proposal almost went so far as to stifle almost any law enforcement intelligence collection and dissemination system. In June of 1975, a bill entitled the Criminal Justice Information Control and Protection of Privacy Act of 1975 was introduced into both houses of Congress. The primary purpose of the bill was to protect the constitutional rights and privacy of individuals upon whom criminal justice information had been collected and to control the collection and dissemination of that and other defined information. The Act was written in such a manner as to regulate the collection and dissemination of certain kinds of information acquired by criminal justice agencies. The information sought to be controlled included what was called Criminal Justice Information, Criminal Justice Investigative Information, and Criminal Justice Intelligence Information. The bill would have required criminal justice agencies to adopt certain procedures designed to protect the collection, access to, and dissemination of criminal justice information. Moreover, the bill would have given a right to individuals to review, and if necessary challenge, the accuracy and completeness of that information.

As to ongoing intelligence operations, the bill would have effectively precluded any organized crime intelligence operations and would have almost completely destroyed any free exchange of information as to those operations among agencies. Fortunately, the bill did not become law, as Congress did not pass that legislation.

Much of the privacy proposals or acts heretofore passed are founded upon seemingly solid and good intended purposes. Past governmental abuses have lead in many instances to these legislative reactions. However, legitimate law enforcement needs to investigate organized crime and its activities must be balanced against the threat of potential privacy invasion as well as the threat posed by organized crime. The need to investigate, uncover, and prosecute organized crime operations cannot be minimized in this regard.

Aside from the potential privacy problems associated with the acquisition, retention, utilization, and dissemination of organized crime intelligence materials, principally upon an interagency basis, other potential problems also arise that must be considered. For example, not all individuals within an agency have a right nor a need to know information contained in organized crime intelligence files. Access to information in those files must accordingly be limited. A permanent procedure for information retention and dissemination must be established so as to control unnecessary and concomitantly risky disclosure of sensitive documents or information. Only those with the need to know as evaluated by the unit head according to established guidelines should be given access to sensitive information and then only according to the permanent procedure developed by the agency.

Information contained in intelligence unit files, particularly items of strategic as opposed to tactical or evidential intelligence, must often be closely guarded not only from unnecessary disclosure but also from abusive discovery proceedings in criminal or civil litigation. Generally, such material will be beyond the scope of most criminal discovery, unless specific allegations are made that particular evidence to be utilized in the criminal trial stems from and is the fruit of illegally and unconstitutionally obtained information of some kind. In this event, subpoenas *duces tecum* (subpoenas for the presence of a particular person with records) or motions for production of documents filed pursuant to suppression motions are often directed at law enforcement agencies seeking information contained in intelligence unit files. Often, the source of information and the method of information acquisition are sought by defense attorneys at the suppression hearing. Remember from Chapter 9 that if this suppression hearing is successful the information will be excluded.

In the event that the evidence to be used by the prosecution at trial stems from the fruits of an illegal seizure of some kind, information as to the acquisition system for that evidence as well as other relevant evidence might come to light. Consequently, intelligence units must keep such information from their case files, inasmuch as collection or retention of that information can be damaging not only to a particular prosecutorial effort but to the entire security of the intelligence system.

Often access to information in intelligence files is sought in the course of civil law suits, where discovery of information is often governed by much broader discovery rules than in criminal trials. Generally, discovery access to information in such situations arises during litigation directed against the agency as a result of its intelligence collection efforts. Often a particular targeted individual may file suit alleging invasion of privacy, violation of civil rights, intentional infliction of emotional distress, and similar tort actions. During the course of that proceeding, discovery attempts generally are made to obtain information held by the intelligence unit as to that particular individual. Such discovery attempts frequently and vigorously are opposed by civil counsel for most agencies and usually with good results in limiting disclosure of sensitive material.

Sometimes, dissemination of intelligence data to other agencies can result in suits for libel, slander, and defamation of character by individuals named in those reports who become aware of the contents of the reports. Prior determination as to the accuracy and reliability of such information as contained in the intelligence unit files is therefore important in the defense of such potential claims, as well as for those internal intelligence evaluation needs, which was discussed in Chapter 11.

As a result of problems involved in the retention and dissemination of information, guidelines must be and have been developed by a number of agencies to govern such procedures. These have been written to principally control the retention and dissemination of information and to minimize some of the problems herein discussed. A variety of examples can be found in *The Intelligence Manual.*

Aside from questions surrounding information storage, retention, and destruction, as well as dissemination of information within an agency or between agencies, the utilization of information is of utmost concern to the intelligence system. The importance of the effective use of such information was recognized in the 1967 President's Crime Commission *Report*, wherein the Commission stated:[8]

> A body of strategic intelligence information would enable agencies to predict what directions organized crime might take, which industries it might try to penetrate, and how it might infiltrate. Law enforcement and regulatory agencies could then develop plans to destroy the organizational framework and coherence of the criminal cartels. Comprehensive strategic planning, however, even with an expanded intelligence effort, will not be possible until relevant disciplines, such as economics, political science, sociology, and operations research, begin to study organized crime intensively.

The development of such information is the highest and best use of the intelligence system, in that it allows for the formulation and implementation of long-range plans to deal with the new and ever increasing threats of organized crime. Moreover, accurate advanced knowledge from such intelligence activities allows for the effective development of enforcement efforts, e.g., undercover operations, such as we discussed in Chapter 11. Additionally, strategic intelligence allows for the consideration and formulation of necessary and effective legislation to deal with the overall and emerging threat of organized crime in advance of widespread problems created by new organized crime activities.

One of the most common uses of intelligence information arises from the development and dissemination of an intelligence report. The intelligence report is the vehicle utilized to transmit an end product of the analytic process. Intelligence reports are of five basic types:[9]

1. *Oral Tactical Response Reports:* These are provided orally, in response to requests for specific information to generally

---

[8]*Report, supra*, Note 1, at 199.

[9]See D. Harris, *Basic Elements of Intelligence*, pp. 66–69 (Washington D.C., September, 1976, rev. ed.).

assist another unit's ongoing investigation.

2. *Written Tactical Response Reports:* These are more detailed written responses to requests for information during ongoing investigations. Typically the reports assess a particular suspect, organization, or the like to assist the tactical unit.

3. *Strategic Reports:* These are written to estimate the overall nature, extent, trends, and patterns of organized crime activities. Assessments are made of the threats, developments, and expected and predicted operations for organized crime. Usually a hypothesis is stated in the report with recommendations for confirming activities and confirming intelligence efforts to be conducted to substantiate the hypothesis. These are comprehensive and sometimes extremely thorough reports used to set high level policy for law enforcement agencies.

4. *Periodic Reports:* These are simple update reports to provide management with status information as to ongoing intelligence investigations.

5. *Prosecutorial Reports:* These are frequently provided for prosecutorial use, concerning matters of evidential intelligence as to a particular case or series of cases. Similar to general case reports used by other enforcement units, these reports are primarily limited to prosecutorial consideration as to initial indictment and prosecution efforts.

The storage, retention, dissemination, and utilization of intelligence information involves a number of considerations. Some of these involve legal questions, some deal with the use of guidelines to preserve the validity of the information, and some pertain to the ultimate use of the information. Different standards, of course, apply as to the utilization of information, particularly when we consider the use of the information for either a tactical or evidential purpose. Once a decision is made however to proceed with prosecution as to a particular group or individual, the utilization of that information must begin to focus on the preparation of a case for ultimate prosecution.

Section IV

Prosecuting Organized Crime Figures

Chapter 14

CASE PREPARATION

Unlike many other criminal prosecutions, prosecutions of organized crime members or groups pose several significant problems: witnesses are often reluctant to testify for fear of organized crime retribution; insiders must often be used to provide testimony against their organized crime compatriots; cooperating witnesses and evidence must be located to provide substantiation for the other testimony to be put forth, most particularly from the insiders; protection must be arranged and provided for the witnesses, often for very extended periods of time; frequently, witnesses must be granted immunity from prosecution before they can be forced or cajoled into cooperation; and lastly, many witnesses who do testify must be given new identities, records, jobs, and the like and then relocated to different areas, under federal or state sponsored witness protection programs. The problems inherent in case preparation, including witness preparation and management, can thus be manifold as well as many faceted.

Once a decision is made to proceed with prosecution of a given individual or group, the investigative focus must shift from its purest form to one of tactical and evidential intelligence gathering. Concentration therefore must be placed upon securing constitutionally obtained and admissible information as well as information otherwise relevant and admissible in the proceeding.

The first step in this directional shift from intelligence gathering to evidence acquisition begins with a so-called "targeting" process. Targeting is simply the identification and selection of the individual or group who will come under intense scrutiny in investigative efforts to compile sufficient evidential intelligence for ultimate use in prosecution against that person or group. The targeting process is more than a guess and is certainly more than wishful thinking. The individual or group to be selected through the targeting process must be selected only after consideration of at least the following factors:

1. What evidential intelligence is already available?
2. How much more such information is necessary for successful prosecution?
3. Are there investigative and evidence gathering tools available to secure the needed and missing information?
4. How much would the acquisition of such information cost?
5. Would other investigative efforts suffer as a result of particular targeting and evidence acquisition efforts and to what degree?
6. Is successful prosecution likely?
7. Would other potential investigative targets have to be granted immunity to secure their cooperation, if necessary, in the prosecution?
8. What are the economic, moral, and actual dangers of the targeted individual or group to the community?
9. How much of an impact upon organized crime would be achieved by successful prosecution?
10. What would be gained from successful prosecution?

After each of these and other factors are considered and addressed in the targeting process as part of the total intelligence process (see Chapter 10), strategies are eventually developed for the evidence acquisition effort. The strategies selected at this level of the investigative process are far different than those overall enforcement strategies that we discussed in preceding chapters regarding intelligence collection, collation, and dissemination. At this level, the strategies to be considered and selected concentrate upon the development and presentation of material for a court prosecution rather than an overall plan to deal with the problem of organized crime over the years.

The strategies for consideration and selection are dependent to varying degrees upon the information that must still be acquired, the activity or group to come under investigation, the ability to acquire the information and through what channels, the availability of witnesses and other evidence, and the likelihood of being able to effectively utilize those witnesses and evidence in a prosecutorial effort in a court of law. For example, in a city without a state wiretapping law, there would be great difficulty in attempting to secure evidential information against a group primarily dependent upon the telephone for their exchange of incriminating information, e.g., a bookmaking operation. In such circumstances, the strategy to be selected for evidence acquisition, of necessity, must exclude efforts to secure incriminating statements contained in such conversations. The focus might then shift to evidence acquisition through surveillance, the use of insiders turned state's witnesses, agents, informers, and/or search warrants. If there would be no way to develop a case against the group without the use of wiretapping, perhaps the strategy would dictate that concentration be placed upon a federal prosecution and cooperation with federal enforcement agencies who have the necessary tools pursuant to Title III to proceed with wiretapping as an evidence acquisition tool.

In any case, the selection of the strategies to be employed must proceed with full realization of the potential and likely problems that can arise in the course of the evidence acquisition process. Limiting or inhibiting factors should be known well in advance of actual acquisition efforts. The normal intelligence system can greatly assist in the strategy selection process at this level. For example, if insider testimony is necessary, such intelligence information is sometimes available about individual's weaknesses, friends, family, health, status within a group, satisfaction with the group, and the like. Upon consideration of all of this information, likely targets for potential witnesses can be more intelligently selected. Often, recruitment of such witnesses can then begin.

In other cases, intelligence information previously acquired can assist in the selection, training, and preparation of an agent for infiltration into a organized crime group for evidence acquisition purposes. Absent such information it would be virtually impossible for any outsider to penetrate any such crime group. Knowledge of the group's behavior, businesses, ventures, and social mores are necessary bits of information to any successful undercover operation.

The screening process of available information already within the system must consequently first take place as a prerequisite to efforts designed to determine what further information is needed. Sometimes there may be enough information; however, in many cases more information must be acquired.

There are a variety of channels through which further information can be acquired for the purposes of fulfilling the investigative evidential intelligence gathering process:

1. Undercover operations staffed with enforcement agents,
2. Informants/Witnesses,
3. Surveillance,
4. Wiretaps or other electronic surveillance,
5. Search warrants, and
6. Grand Jury Proceedings.

Although we discussed the first four of these methods in Chapter 11, it should be clear that the focus would shift in such operations once the decision has been made to prosecute. Specific evidential information would become the target rather than broader knowledge or information.

Search warrants are an excellent evidential acquisition tool, generally used in the final stages of an investigation focused on ultimate prosecution. Search warrants are obtained utilizing an application, an affidavit or affidavits, and such other testimony or exhibits as may be required to establish the existence of probable cause. Probable cause, although not precisely defined, is generally regarded as being established from facts or apparent facts that when taken together provide a reasonable basis for belief that a crime has been or is being committed and that there is something connected with that violation of law on the premises or the person to be searched. The information necessary to obtain the search warrant may be graphically depicted as shown in Figure 16.

The search warrant can be issued only by a judge, assuming he is convinced and finds the existence of probable cause. Once issued, the search warrant is directed to a law enforcement officer for execution so that the place or person described may be searched. Generally, a time limit is established for the execution of the warrant, e.g., one to three days, to insure that the finding of probable cause will remain fresh.

Search warrants, once validly issued, act as keys of sorts to allow

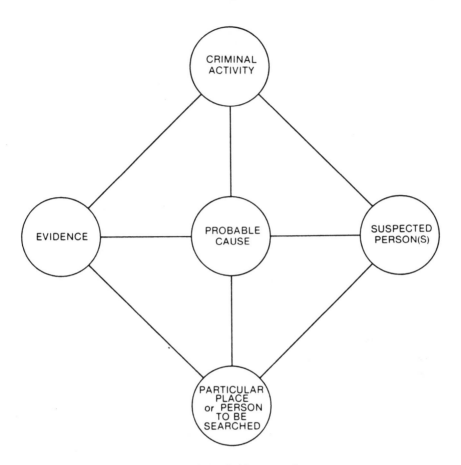

Figure 16. Probable cause chart.

entry into the place or onto the person to be searched that would otherwise be inaccessible to law enforcement. Typically the search warrant execution process proceeds on a systematic, room-by-room basis to insure acquisition of all important and relevant evidence. Evidence so seized is usually viewed by the judge issuing the warrant and then stored to await trial use. Relevant and material evidence thus acquired in the search warrant procedure often can greatly assist in organized crime prosecutions.

Necessary information for the acquisition of the search warrant is generally obtained through the use of undercover operations, surveillance, electronic surveillance, wiretaps, and/or informants. Hearsay may be used to help establish probable cause to secure the warrant. Extreme and technical rules have heretofore applied as to the use of informants in the search warrant application process. The operation of these rules has been somewhat dependent upon the type of informer utilized.

There are three basic types of informers when considering the search warrant application process:

1. *Identifiable Informants,* e.g., victims of crime, ordinary witnesses, good citizens, any of whom's name and identity can be used in the affidavit for the search warrant;
2. *Confidential Informants,* e.g., those persons supplying information whose names and identities must be protected so as to avoid exposing them to risks of harm or death; and
3. *Anonymous Informants,* e.g., those whose identities are unknown.

The use of hearsay acquired from such informants in the search warrant acquisition process to assist in establishing probable cause is quite commonplace. However, since the search warrant process is subject to constitutional constraints, specific rules have governed the use of this hearsay. Prior to 1983, specific and rigid tests developed by the Supreme Court in *Aguilar v. Texas*, 378 U.S. 108 (1964), and *Spinelli v. United States*, 393 U.S. 410 (1969), applied so as to require not only a "factual basis" for such hearsay information but also verification or corroboration of that hearsay information as well in the search warrant application process. Significant changes in these requirements were made in the recent case of *Illinois v. Gates*, 103 S. Ct. 2317 (1983), where the United States Supreme Court reconsidered its prior rulings and adopted a less stringent standard for considering and evaluating hearsay testimony, known as the totality of the circumstances rule. Under this newly promulgated rule, a court reviewing the warrant procurement process will be required to consider the total facts and circumstances presented prior to issuing any warrant to meet the Fourth Amendment requirements of independent evaluation by a Judge or Magistrate and determination of the presence or absence of probable cause for the issuance of such a search warrant. Under this new rule, the court will not be bound to consider hearsay evidence by stringent standards as set by the *Aguilar* and *Spinelli* cases.

Pursuant to the rule adopted by the Court in *Illinois u Gates*, a Magistrate considering the issuance of a search warrant based upon hearsay information is required only to make a practical, commonsense determination as to the presence or absence of probable cause to believe that evidence is located in a particular place or on a particular person to be searched. Although independent police corroboration of hearsay information is still of significant value, no rigid test as heretofore developed by the Court in previous holdings will be followed. Henceforth, all facts and circumstances underlying the acquisition of the information and the means and methods of information evaluation will be considered by the court in the search warrant process.

Aside from the use of the search warrant process for evidence acquisition, evidential intelligence is often acquired through the use of regular or special investigative grand juries. The 1967 President's Crime Commission found in it's *Report:*

> A compulsory process is necessary to obtain essential testimony or material. This is most readily accomplished by an investigative grand jury or an alternate mechanism through which the attendance of witnesses and production of books and records can be ordered. Such grand juries must stay in session long enough to allow for the unusually long time required to build an organized crime case.[1]

The Commission recommended the impanelling of such investigative grand juries at least annually in each jurisdiction with major organized crime activity.[2] The power of a grand jury and its usefulness in organized crime investigations has been very vividly described:

> [A] grand jury is awesome. The right of subpoena vests it with power that no detective or agent can legitimately wield. The threat of perjury prosecutions can cajole timid witnesses into giving information which would otherwise remain hidden. When a witness is immunized, under a proper statute, he can be coerced into telling all he knows with the threat of

---

[1]The President's Commission on Law Enforcement and Administration of Justice, *The Challenge of Crime in a Free Society: A Report*, p. 200 (Washington D.C. 1967).

[2]*Id*

contempt proceedings. Perhaps most importantly, the psychological effect of being called before the grand jury, of being summoned to answer questions in solemn surroundings before ordinary citizens—this can unnerve the most hardened capo in La Cosa Nostra.[3]

Grand jury proceedings are secret, generally one-sided presentations designed to secure and consider evidence of the commission of criminal activity to determine whether there is probable cause to indict, or formally charge, individuals with violations of criminal law. The process is nonadversarial and often rigidly controlled by the prosecutors presenting the facts to the grand jury. The process has been the subject of much criticism because of alleged overzealous use of the proceedings, its nonadversarial form, its secretive proceedings, its intimidation of witnesses in some respects, its questioning methods for some witnesses, even potential defendants, without the presence of counsel for such witnesses, and its issuance of reports sometimes without accompanying indictment. However, the grand jury indictment process for capital and infamous crimes (most felonies) is constitutionally mandated by the Fifth Amendment of the United States Constitution.[4]

At the federal level, Title I of the Organized Crime Control Act of 1970 created special federal grand juries in certain established jurisdictions as well as in areas where the attorney general or his deputy made application to a district judge for the creation of a special grand jury because of criminal activity in those areas. These Title I grand juries are required to sit at least once every eighteen months and may continue their business for eighteen months after being convened unless granted a six-month extension by the court.

Title I specifically authorizes such grand juries, by majority vote, to issue a report, "Concerning non-criminal misconduct, malfeasance, or misfeasance in office involving organized criminal activity by an appointed public officer or employee (federal, state or territorial) as the basis for a recommendation of removal

---

[3]Remarks of Wilhom S. Lynch to L.E.A.A. Conference, Norman, Oklahoma, March 4, 1970, reported in The National Association of Attorneys General, *Organized Crime Control Legislation*, p. 117 (Raleigh, North Carolina 1975).

[4]U.S. Constitution, Amendment V (1791): "No person shall be held to answer for a capital, or otherwise infamous crime, unless on a presentment or indictment of a Grand Jury . . . "

or disciplinary actions; or, regarding organized crime conditions in the district."[5]

If the district court is satisfied that the report to be issued by a grand jury is supported by a preponderance of the evidence and otherwise authorized by law, it is filed as a public record. Anyone named therein must have had an opportunity, however, to testify personally and through a reasonable number of witnesses before the grand jury as a prerequisite to the publication of his or her name in the report. Each such person must also be given a copy of the report and each has twenty days to respond thereto prior to the report's filing with the court. Responses, if any, become an appendix to the report, unless otherwise excluded by the judge.

Some states have developed similar investigative grand juries principally on statewide levels, but these states are in the definite minority. All states, however, have grand jury procedures to review and consider evidence of criminal activity. Sometimes in the course of these proceedings, the focus will concentrate on organized crime activities. In such situations, although limited by time, jurisdiction, and sometimes the court, much information can be obtained that will assist the intelligence process as well as any ultimate prosecution.

The normal grand jury system operates by subpoenaing witnesses before it and then examining those witnesses to illicit testimony. From that evidence, decisions are made by the grand jury as a body to indict or not to indict given individuals for criminal activity.

Often, the grand jury, through its subpoena power, can obtain records for ultimate prosecutorial use at trial. Many of these records would not otherwise be available to the state. The records that can be obtained include medical records, otherwise unavailable without a medical release or subpoena because of the doctor/patient privilege, telephone toll records, which are listings of all long distance telephone calls placed from a given number by date and time, employment records, some tax returns, and utility bills and similar financial documents that may be used for financial analysis as we discussed in Chapter 12. Although some information is

---

[5]18 U.S.C. §3333 (1970).

beyond subpoena, e.g., certain federally acquired or maintained information protected by federal privacy laws, much valuable information can be obtained through the grand jury's subpoena power. Much of this information can be used directly in later prosecution or in the intelligence system after analysis and comparison with other bits of stored or acquired information.

At the grand jury level, many witnesses, particularly those associated with organized crime, claim the privilege against self-incrimination pursuant to the Fifth Amendment to the United States Constitution (see Chapter 9). In these situations, specific procedures to overcome that assertion have developed.

In the eventuality that a determination is made that the testimony of a grand jury witness is necessary, the prosecution will extensively question the witness in the presence of the grand jury. If the witness is concerned with providing self-incriminating answers, he will claim the Fifth Amendment privilege to all or most questions. Once the examination is completed, the transcript of that questioning is typed up and presented with a motion to the presiding judge of the grand jury whereby the prosecution asks the court to determine whether or not the privilege may be properly applied to each question asked of the witness. The court will then examine each question and the concommitant claim of constitutional privilege. Once that determination is made, the court will issue an order, directing the witness to answer those questions the judge determined were nonincriminating. The witness would then be brought back before the grand jury and those questions found permissible by the court would be repeated to the witness. In the eventuality that the witness would still refuse to answer, the prosecution would take the witness before the court and upon motion ask the court to find the witness in contempt. If, after inquiry by the court, the witness still refuses to answer the questions previously found by the judge to be nonincriminating, the court will often find the witness in contempt, and the witness can be lawfully incarcerated in many cases until he purges himself of contempt, i.e., answers the questions.

If the prosecution determines that the testimony of any witness is necessary and the witness claims the Fifth Amendment privilege set forth above, the prosecution will often petition the court overseeing the grand jury to grant the witness immunity from prosecution. In the event that the judge grants the immunity, and the grant is coextensive with the privilege it replaces (see Chapter 9), the witness through the contempt power of the court can be compelled to testify.

Aside from the acquisition of witnesses through this procedure, other witnesses often come forward to provide testimony voluntarily or after some preliminary discussions with the prosecution. Often, it is necessary, even with witnesses who have been granted immunity and then compelled to testify, to provide extensive protection for them from organized crime retaliation and retribution. The protection afforded such witnesses is sometimes not limited to grand jury or trial but on occasion must extend for years afterward or even for the lifetime of the witness. The federal government has been most active in this area as compared to state governments.

In 1970, as part of the Organized Crime Control Act, the Attorney General, in Title V of the Act, was authorized to provide for witness protection in organized crime cases. The Act empowered the Attorney General to:

> provide for the health, safety and welfare of witnesses and persons . . . and the families of witnesses and persons intended to be called as Government witnesses in legal proceedings instituted against any person alleged to have participated in an organized criminal activity whenever, in his judgement, testimony from, or willingness to testify by, such a witness would place his life or person, or the life or person of a member of his family or household, in jeopardy. Any person availing himself of an offer by the Attorney General to use such facilities may continue to use such facilities for as long as the Attorney General determines the jeopardy to his life or person continues.[6]

The federal government as well as various state governments have had witnesses participate in this program. Over 3500 witnesses have participated in the program since 1970 along with approximately 9,000 family members. Typically, witnesses who enter the program, as well as members of their family, are closely guarded and protected through grand jury and trial proceedings. Following trial, they are often relocated to another part of the country,

---

[6]P.L. 91-452, 84 Stat. 922, Title V, §502 (1970).

given new identities, documents, and jobs to assist them in their new assumed lives. However, despite the program's general success rate there have been some problems.

About one-fourth to one-third of all participants eventually drop out of the program and sometimes turn back to criminal activity. Some must relocate more than one time because of breaches of confidentiality or recognition of their true identities.

The program, commonly known as the Witness Protection and Security Program, is administered by the U.S. Marshall's Office. Much criticism has been directed at the program and the Marshall's management of it for alleged abuses including failure to provide new identities, documents, jobs, credit histories, and backgrounds; failure to live up to promises; failure to properly protect and transport or assist the protected witnesses; and even assisting noncustodial parents in alleged "child stealing" activities.[7]

Recently the program has undergone some internal improvements because of the continuing need for an effective and efficient witness protection program. Through the cooperation of the United States Chamber of Commerce, over 150 major companies now assist in providing jobs for protected and relocated witnesses. Cooperation among some of the various state and federal agencies necessary to obtain new identities and documents, e.g., social security cards, drivers licenses, etc., for witnesses is improving but still fraught with some problems. Moreover, marshalls are now better trained and more sensitized to the needs of their protected charges.

Although states can participate in the federal program by payment for their witnesses' maintenance, not many have availed themselves of this opportunity upon a frequent basis. Few states have similar programs themselves, although some clearly recognize the need.[8]

Witness protection programs, despite some serious shortcomings,

---

[7]See e.g., Long, "The Government Stole My Son!" *Family Weekly*, p. 6 (July 19, 1981); Press and Shannon, "Life in Hiding," part of "The New Mafia," *Newsweek Magazine*, p. 42 (January 5, 1981).

[8]The Law Enforcement Consulting Committee, *Report to the Governor of Ohio on Organized Crime*, p. xvi (Columbus, Ohio 1982); Pennsylvania Crime Commission, *A Decade of Organized Crime: 1980 Report*, p. xii (St. Davids, Pennsylvania, 1980).

do assist in the organized crime prosecution effort, often with very successful results. Quite recently, an insider, Aladena "Jimmy the Weasel" Fratianno, provided testimony from one coast to the other against alleged Cosa Nostra figures. Like his famous but lower eschelon predecessor, Joseph Valachi, Fratianno has exposed some of the most innerworkings of the Mafia and will undoubtedly stay in the witness protection program the remainder of his life. Without this program, the probabilities of securing such testimony would have been very small if not impossible.

Although most states do not have formal witness protection programs, prosecutors do typically provide protective custody for witnesses used in organized crime and conspiracy trials and often will assist witnesses in efforts to relocate after trial. If they have been involved in criminal activities, prosecutors may assist them in obtaining probation, parole, or secure quarters in penal institutions. While not as effective or formal as the federal witness protection plan, such local prosecutorial assistance is commonplace.

The immunity/contempt process as well as the witness protection and security programs greatly assist case preparation activities of law enforcement. Other methods of witness acquisition are much less frequently used and are generally not as successful. While witnesses do sometimes come forward, voluntarily and without prosecutorial or law enforcement cajoling or pressure, it is not commonplace. Usually cases must be built from information at hand or from evidence acquired after targeting efforts for witness selection.

Sometimes, as we discussed in Chapter 11, undercover operations with law enforcement agents can be successful depending upon the purpose of the infiltration. For the most part, the longer the period of agent infiltration and the higher his penetration, the more likely a successful case can be prepared, but it is also true that his chances of exposure will greatly increase at the same time. However, most agent infiltration programs do not last for any extended length of time. Moreover, if extended infiltration takes place, the greater is the hardship to the agent and his or her family due to long absences and great risks. In 1982 and 1983, a six-year-long FBI agent's infiltration into very high levels of Cosa Nostra was publicly revealed. Although, for the most part, the agent's early years of infiltration must have been directed more at strategic intelligence gathering activities rather than evidential intelligence gathering activities, the end result of his infiltration resulted in prosecutions of high members of La Cosa Nostra and the final purpose of his penetration must have been to focus on evidential intelligence gathering activities. Such infiltrations, however, are rare and difficult.

Through the use of search warrants, informers/witnesses, agents, and grand jury proceedings, evidence is prepared and secured for use at trial. Coupled with eavesdropping and electronic surveillance evidence, if available, the case is now set for prosecution, the next and final result of evidential intelligence gathering activities.

♦

Chapter 15

COURT PROSECUTION OF
ORGANIZED CRIME FIGURES

Prosecution of organized crime members can be much more difficult than prosecution of other criminal defendants. Typically, organized crime members have teams of lawyers as well as accountants and other expert witnesses to assist them in the defense of their cases. Often, several such organized crime defendants are on trial together, where the charges include one or more counts of conspiracy together with one or more substantive charges. Moreover, cases against organized crime members typically involve a great deal of circumstantial evidence together with co-conspirator testimony from a former organized crime member turned state's witness. Frequently, such individuals come under scathing defense attack because of their own criminal backgrounds. They are often consequently difficult to present, manage, and display to the jury.

Particular problems frequently arise in the course of organized crime prosecutions. Some of these deal with time elements, evidence and procedure, and the tactics to be used during trial. For example, trials of most organized crime members are quite lengthy and often involve many counts of illegal behavior, including conspiracy. Generally the trial of such persons is preceded by much publicity in the local media. Selection of a fair, impartial, and unbiased jury may be greatly hampered as a result of such pre-trial publicity. Jurors scheduled for these cases must frequently undergo very severe hardships because of the attention such organized crime cases bring as well as the length of many specific organized crime trials.

In order to properly address and examine each stage of trial and the particular problems associated with those stages, it is best to examine the prosecutorial process chronologically.

201

Pre-Trial

ARREST, ARRAIGNMENT, BAIL, PRE-TRIAL, GAG ORDERS:
Several very important matters must be considered after indictment but before trial. Inasmuch as the grand jury indictment
process is secretive, the very first news the media will usually
obtain is upon the arrest of the organized crime figures after the
indictment is made public. Typically, the organized crime figure
will be apprehended and taken before a judge or magistrate for
arraignment on the charges and for the purpose of appointing
counsel if necessary and the posting of bond.

This stage can be very critical in several respects. The right to
post bail is guaranteed by the United States Constitution as well as
various state constitutions, and most scheduled bond amounts
normally posted in serious felony cases easily could be made by
many organized crime figures; as a consequence, the purpose of
bail (to insure presence at all court proceedings) would not be
achieved by the posting of a relatively small bond amount, especially in large-scale drug cases. In such cases bail in the hundreds
of thousands of dollars is not uncommon and certainly not unreasonable. Frequently, prosecutors will push for the setting of
high bails on organized crime cases for these very reasons. Such
moves are often countered by defense counsel efforts to downplay
their clients involvement, show their client's ties to and respectability in the community, their status and employment, and sometimes even their ill health, all in an effort to secure release pending
trial on a low bond amount. (This latter "ill health" argument is
frequently used, and often with success by higher-up organized
crime members, who if convicted, also use this method to avoid or
lessen harsh and otherwise unpleasant sentences.)

Judges or magistrates, when setting bail, frequently use predetermined schedules for such bail amounts and add to or subtract
from those schedules depending upon a variety of circumstances
including the seriousness of the crime, the employment, property
ownership, status, and contacts of the defendant with and in the
community, the dollars if any involved in the particular crime,
past criminal records, family ties, the likelihood that the defendant
will flee or stay for prosecution, and many more relevant factors.

Many organized crime members can favorably meet most of these considerations so as to achieve low bail amounts.

Sometimes at this stage of the proceedings or shortly thereafter either the prosecutor and/or the defense attorney will ask for appropriate "gag" orders to be issued by the court. These gag orders are designed to keep the parties (the litigants), the police, and others from discussing the case so that the dangers of pre-trial publicity are lessened. In this manner, the chance of picking an untainted jury, which is free of bias, prejudice, or preconceived notions, will be greatly increased.

DISCOVERY, PRE-TRIAL MOTIONS, AND PRE-TRIAL PROCEEDINGS: Prior to trial, each side in a civil or criminal proceeding is given the opportunity, pursuant to court rule or statute, to learn what witnesses, evidence, tangible objects, and the like the other side has and intends to introduce at time of trial. In a criminal case, the discovery demands and responsibilities are greater upon the prosecution than the defense. Often the prosecution cannot obtain any evidence from the defense until the government has first complied with the defendant's request for discovery. Often the defendant can also obtain what is called a "Bill of Particulars" from the state upon request, which requires the prosecution to state where, when, and under what particular circumstances the charged criminal act was committed. Frequently, with a many-count indictment, this can be quite time-consuming for the prosecution.

At this stage of the proceeding in organized crime cases, many prosecutors frequently refuse to disclose the names or identities of their witnesses. Most state statutes, or rules of criminal procedure, allow the prosecution to refuse to disclose the names and identities of certain witnesses when the prosecution certifies that disclosure of these witnesses would probably jeopardize their safety or well-being or that of their families.

Pursuant to the Federal Rules of Civil Procedure, protective orders are available from normal disclosure rules of discovery. Typically, state rules also make such provision.

In civil proceedings the most common method of discovery is through the use of depositions, the taking of out-of-court testimony under oath in the presence of a court reporter. In criminal proceedings the right to pre-trial deposition discovery is very limited and consequently little utilized.

A variety of pre-trial motions designed to acquire discoverable information are often utilized in the course of discovery. The purposes for these motions might be severalfold as we shall see. These motions typically include the following:

(a) *Motions for grand jury transcripts:* Often, requests for transcripts of the testimony of witnesses before grand juries are sought to learn the identities of such witnesses and their testimony in advance of trial. Absent certain well-defined circumstances, often completed by in camera (in chambers) inspections by the court, these transcripts because of the secretive nature of the grand jury proceedings are not available.

(b) *Motions for inspection, testing, and/or copying of documents, papers, effects, and similar bits of documentary or physical evidence to be used at time of trial:* Frequently, much tangible, real evidence and documentary evidence is used in organized crime prosecutions. Defendants have the right to inspect and copy or photograph such evidence, and in an appropriate case, such defendants may obtain expert testing or analysis of the evidence itself, such as with drugs or weapons.

(c) *Motions to Suppress Evidence:* Suppression motions are one of the most commonly filed pleadings in criminal trial practice. The motion generally seeks to exclude evidence from trial consideration because of claims that such evidence was obtained in violation of constitutional, legislative, or judicial requirements. Motions to suppress are often directed at excluding evidence that is claimed to have been obtained in violation of the Fourth, Fifth, and/or Fourteenth Amendments to the United States Constitution and/or similar state constitutional protections. Typically, motions to suppress seek to exclude damaging physical or documentary evidence, contraband, or incriminating statements. Certain distinct procedures apply at this stage.

Typically, since the motion is filed by the defense, the defense must proceed first with evidence, although the burden of proof is upon the government to establish the admissibility of evidence and the fact that it was obtained in accordance with law. The defendants pursuing this course are given the opportunity of testifying for the limited purposes of the suppression hearing, and if any such testimony is given, that testimony, although subject to prosecutorial cross-examination, is not subject to use or comment later at any trial. The justification for this rule lies in the rationale embodied in the Fourth, Fifth, and Fourteenth Amendments to the United States Constitution. If the prosecution does not meet its burden at this stage, the evidence and perhaps any fruits of the evidence as well will be excluded from trial (see Chapter 9). It is at this stage where the so-called "exclusionary rule" discussed in Chapter 9 comes to life and operation.

(d) *Motions In Limine:* Motions in limine are frequently filed in both criminal and civil proceedings and seek to limit and/or exclude certain evidence from jury consideration. The defense frequently seeks to exclude potentially prejudicial matters or evidence by this motion such as gruesome pictures or statements that might inflame a jury, certain prejudicial comments that a witness may say, including references to the Mafia, La Cosa Nostra, The Black Hand, or similar comments, evidence of a defendants past criminal background, and many other factors.

(e) *Motions to Dismiss Charges:* Sometimes in the course of criminal proceedings, including organized crime prosecutions, motions are filed to dismiss pending criminal charges for a variety of reasons. These may be predicated upon an alleged improperly impaneled grand jury that returned the indictment, a statute of limitations defense, prosecutorial or law enforcement misconduct, defects in the charges, or a host of other reasons.

(f) *Motions to Sequester the Jury:* Often, in organized crime or capital cases, motions to sequester jurors are made by the prosecution and/or the defense to insure the jurors will remain unaffected by media publicity during trial. In organized crime cases, moreover, it is much more frequently asked for by the prosecution because of fear of jury tampering or threats.

Prior to trial, the court in almost all cases will call the attorneys together at a pre-trial hearing designed really to keep the court's hands in the proceeding and to make sure the case is commencing as it should. Pre-trial hearings are used to limit the issues, seek resolution of cases, discuss problems likely to occur, and generally insure the proper management of the case. It is at this stage that most plea-bargaining takes place. The formality of pre-trials varies greatly with the particular jurisdiction, but the purpose is almost always the same. If the pretrial doesn't result in some resolution of the case, it moves on to trial.

Trial

The trial procedure for any criminal case, including organized crime prosecutions, follows a certain, preset order:

1. Voir Dire (Jury Selection);
2. Opening statements by the attorneys;
3. Prosecution's presentation of its Case in Chief;
4. Defense Case in Chief;
5. Rebuttal;
6. Sur-Rebuttal;
7. Opening prosecutorial argument to jury;
8. Defense argument to jury;
9. Closing prosecutorial argument to jury;
10. Instructions to the jury by the court;
11. Deliberations by the jury; and
12. Verdict and Sentencing.

At each stage of the trial procedure, problems often arise, some of which are more particularly relevant to organized crime prosecutions than others. To these we now turn.

VOIR DIRE. The voir dire stage of trial, or the jury selection process, centers upon counsel's efforts to question a panel of prospective jurors to determine if a fair and impartial jury, free of prejudices (prejudgements) and biases, can be selected to hear the case. Often, because of the notoriety of most organized crime cases, many jurors have heard or read something about the case in one of the local medias. This can make selection of jurors difficult if the media coverage has given them information that has or would strongly affect the jurors' ability to be fair and impartial. If jurors cannot indicate an ability to be fair and impartial because of such coverage, they will be excluded from further jury consideration and asked to step down from the prospective jury panel *for cause*. In the event that it becomes apparent that the entire pool of prospective jurors has become tainted to the point that selection of a fair and impartial panel is impossible, the motion for change of venue, or the request to transfer the case to another jurisdiction, would be in order. Such motions are sometimes made at the pre-trial stage, but the proper time for the motion is during voir dire, while efforts are underway to select the jury. Prior to that stage there is usually insufficient evidence to indicate that a fair and impartial jury cannot be selected unless extensive community surveys have been scientifically and properly taken that without question indicate large-scale community infection because of pre-trial publicity making the probable selection of a fair and impartial jury impossible.

Prospective jurors who demonstrate other prejudices during voir dire will also be examined and excused for cause from the panel. Frequently, in organized crime prosecutions once it becomes clear that the case will proceed against alleged Mafia members or La Cosa Nostra members, some jurors will express an unwillingness to serve. Moreover, oftentimes because of a pre-trial decision to sequester jurors in some cases, jurors at this stage may indicate an unwillingness to sit for extended periods because of young children, employment, health, or other valid reasons. Although it is much more difficult today to be excused from jury duty, similar problems often result in a juror's exclusion from the panel. Once a panel is selected following examination and excuses for cause, a limited number of preemptory challenges are given to each side (challenges for any reason causing a juror to be excused) following which, the jury is impanelled and sworn in. Often, especially for trials likely to continue for some time, several alternate jurors are seated to ensure, that if some misfortune befalls one or more of the members of the jury panel, that a replacement who has heard the evidence can step in and continue the previous member's duties.

EVIDENCE PRESENTATION. Frequent problems and special situations occur at this stage to the government in the presentation of its case and the selection and use of witnesses as well as evidence. Many practical considerations also abound in trials of organized crime cases. Of the problems occurring at this stage the following are most frequent.

Recalcitrant Witnesses — Frequently witnesses who have testified in grand jury or who have given sworn statements to the prosecution prior to trial forget for a variety of reasons many salient, important facts. A prosecutor calling such witnesses is limited to a large degree as to what he can do to correct this forgetfulness. The prosecution as to its witnesses is limited to conducting what's called "direct examination" in its questioning of that witness. Direct examination is a questioning of the witness that does not suggest or imply an answer in the question itself, such as "What is your name?" which is a direct examination question, as compared to "Isn't it true that your name is John Jones?" which is an objectionable direct examination question inasmuch as an answer is suggested in the question. These direct examination rules have developed procedurally for a variety of reasons, including the most obvious of which is letting the witness tell the facts his way so that a truer and more accurate picture may be presented to the jury.

Witnesses whose memories fade at this stage cause much concern and trouble for the prosecution. The prosecution cannot lead the witness in questioning, although he can attempt to rehabilitate the witness by refreshing his memory through the use of prior statements. Sometimes such refreshment tactics do not work.

Witnesses Who Change their Testimony — Sometimes, especially in organized crime prosecutions, a witness or witnesses may be called to the stand and testify completely or significantly different from prior grand jury testimony or similar pre-trial statements under oath. Stories in such cases can significantly change much to the chagrin of the prosecution. Through a claim of "surprise" the prosecution in certain circumstances can ask the court for permission to cross-examine the witness. Although such a procedure if allowed is often designed to assist the truth finding process and to discover possible perjury, many jurisdictions do not allow the prosecution under any circumstances to conduct a cross-examination of its own witnesses. In those jurisdictions, the prosecution is limited or prevented altogether from bringing out the truth from such witnesses. Frequently, the prosecution can obtain through answers to somewhat innocuous questions enough information to serve as the groundwork for a later perjury charge against the witness.

Expert Witnesses—Expert witnesses must be frequently used in organized crime prosecutions. Such witnesses, unlike lay people, are allowed to express opinions regarding certain matters because of their experience, training, or education. While experts may not testify as to ultimate issues (i.e., is the defendant guilty of the crime charged?), such witnesses are of great practical assistance to the entire system of criminal and civil justice. Typically, doctors, dentists, accountants, engineers, metallurgists, scientists, and a host of others are allowed to testify and express opinions about various evidentiary matters that are within their areas of expertise. In organized crime prosecutions, voice print identification experts, scientists and qualified lab technicians, ballistic experts, and accountants are frequently used to provide testimony. Accountants are of unique benefit in providing explanatory information regarding the books and records of organized crime operations, particularly as to bookmaking and other gambling groups, drug rings, and infiltrations into legitimate business. The net worth method that we discussed in Chapter 12 is used at this stage in court by the expert witness to provide information as to the earnings of an organized crime group or member. The method has been used frequently and with much success in income tax evasion prosecutions.

Evidentiary Rules in Conspiracy Cases

Co-Conspirators—Many organized crime indictments often involve at least one count charging conspiratorial conduct, by which several defendants are charged with reaching an agreement to commit a criminal act. Evidentially, one conspirator may not be convicted upon the basis of another co-conspirator's testimony alone. There must be some evidence that corroborates the co-conspirator's testimony or the prosecution must fail for a lack of sufficient proof.

Evidence of Prior Criminal Activity—Evidence of prior criminal activity or reputation of a defendant is generally not admissible in a current prosecution including organized crime cases. However, there are certain well-defined exceptions to this rule. Evidence of prior criminal conduct is often admissible to prove one or more of the elements of the current criminal charge such as motive, identity, absence of mistake or accident, or to show the existence of a scheme, plan, or conspiracy. If used for such purposes, evidence of prior crimes or criminal conduct is often admissible, not to show that the defendant is a bad or criminal man but rather to show one or more of the elements of the currently indicted crime. Although such proof has sometimes been subject to prosecutorial abuse, it is extremely relevant and material evidence in a proper case.

Absent such elements being in issue, evidence of past criminal or bad conduct is not admissible unless the defendant's character is put in issue (by the defense, in its Case in Chief), by offers of evidence of good character, or when the defendant testifies and the prosecution questions him about past felony or criminal activities for the purposes of impeachment. Once evidence of the defendant's past is put into issue by the defendant, the prosecution is then free to present evidence of bad character, which would include evidence of past criminal conduct. Moreover, once the defendant testifies, he opens his background for prosecutorial attack, which would include the right to ask the defendant about past criminal activities for impeachment purposes.

Practical Considerations at Work During Trial

EVIDENCE PRESENTATION. Various practical considerations must be considered in the trial of organized crime figures. Typically, an insider turned state witness or an informer will testify in the prosecution's case. These individuals will often be subject to scathing cross-examination in efforts to discredit them and their testimony. Such attacks will center upon the promises that have been made to such witnesses by the prosecution, the deals that have been struck with such witnesses, the favors or payments that have been made to sustain these witnesses, the sometimes infamous or criminal backgrounds of the witnesses, and their past friendly relationships with the defendants, thereby demonstrating their Judas behavior in testifying, perhaps for hidden, jealous, or self-interest reasons.

Such cross-examination tactics can greatly discredit these witnesses, whose testimony must often be minutely corroborated to make it believable. Efforts must be put forth by prosecutors in such situations to make these witnesses as believable and credible as possible to the jury.

Through the process of trial of organized crime members, prosecutors are frequently mindful of the need to maintain tight control over their witnesses for fear that they will be approached by the organized crime member on trial or his compatriots. The close management and control of these witnesses during trial is important. Witness coordinators are often used for this purpose within prosecutor's offices. Moreover, prosecutors must also be watchful for efforts to tamper with the jury panel, especially if the panel is not sequestered by court order.

Frequent efforts are made in many trials of organized crime members when several are tried together, to separate the upper-eschelon members from those others who can be willingly sacrificed for trial. Prosecutors often have great difficulty when proceeding in such cases. Combined and cooperative efforts made between various defendants to ensure that the focus of the prosecution remains upon certain defendants can greatly hurt the prosecutor's case. If these lower-level defendants testify, efforts must concentrate, among other things, upon their continuing contacts and associations with the upper-level defendants and their receipt of instructions from them. Wiretaps or electronic surveillance evidence if available can be used for this purpose.

ARGUMENT. Organized crime trials can be very complex and can last several weeks or even months. Hundreds of witnesses and exhibits may be put forth before the jury for factual determination. Argument is often critical in tying together all of the facets of such trials.

Some of the techniques used in the intelligence process can also assist the prosecution at this stage of trial. Of particular importance in organized crime conspiracy trials is the use of link network analysis. In such trials, proof of the existence of a criminal conspiracy comes from a variety of evidentiary sources. Unless these bits of evidentiary information are tied together in a cohesive and comprehensive fashion, the jury may be unable to see the total picture. The prosecution, therefore, must be able to effectively tie the evidence together in such a way that will enable the jury to see the interrelationships between the various persons making up the criminal syndicate. Link network analysis techniques, discussed in Chapter 12, can also aid the prosecution during trial and in argument to the jury.

In the course of trial, the analysis techniques as displayed to the jury can assist in graphically demonstrating relationships between individuals. The use of such visual aids along with oral arguments can greatly increase the learning process for the jury and in the process assist the prosecution's Case in Chief.

CONCLUSION

Prosecution of organized crime figures are difficult, time-consuming propositions. Attention to law and evidence, practical considerations, and trial techniques are all critical to successful prosecution.

Chapter 16

SENTENCING

The sentencing of a convicted organized crime member is one of the most crucial stages in the administration of justice, as well as the culmination of much law enforcement effort. The sentencing process as to these individuals raises several complex and often competing issues, the resolution of which is sometimes very elusive.

Sentencing is usually an entirely subjective process, entrusted to the judiciary, and as such lends itself to extremely wide latitude in the interpretation of information used for sentencing purposes. The information used as the basis for most sentencing decisions is often limited to the facts presented at trial or derived from police and/or prosecutor reports. In addition, presentence reports, prepared by the court's probation department, are often heavily relied upon by most courts involved in making sentencing decisions. From such limited information, the court is called upon to impose an appropriate sentence or to predict the future outcome of a defendant's behavior in the course of granting probation to that defendant. The judge's determination is often expected to support the goals of the criminal justice system, conform to the local communities' contemporary standards, and protect the rights of the defendant. Although this is a difficult task even in more ordinary criminal cases such as murder, rape, robbery, and other street crimes, it is almost impossible to perform in admittedly complex and often ambiguous organized crime cases.

Sentencing decisions are also difficult in certain other respects, inasmuch as many questions abound in sentencing, and many diverse and competing factors must often be considered. Some of these problems arise from the very nature of the sentencing process, while others stem from the character of the criminal activity.

One of the most long-standing sentencing problems in orga-

214 of Corporations of Corruption: A Systematic Study of Organized Crime

nized crime cases has arisen from an inability to appropriately punish organized criminal conduct as compared to other criminal acts. In 1967, the President's Crime Commission reported in this regard as follows: "Criminal statutes do not now authorize greater punishment when the violation was committed as part of an organized crime business."[1]

The Commission ultimately recommended that "Federal and State legislation should be enacted to provide for extended prison terms where the evidence, presentence report, or sentencing hearing shows that a felony was committed as part of a continuing illegal business in which the convicted offender occupied a supervisory or other management position."[2]

Similar findings or recommendations have also been made at the state level. For example, in 1980, The Pennsylvania Crime Commission reported:

> Sentencing for organized crime figures should take into account their long involvement in criminal activities.
>
> The Commission has neither the right nor the desire to instruct sentencing judges on the exercise of judicial discretion. Nevertheless, a successful prosecution of an organized criminal is the result of an intense and prolonged effort accomplished against almost insurmountable odds. When finally convicted, the sentence should reflect their long-standing involvement in criminal activities.[3]

Such findings are not isolated among any of the informed states. Sentencing statutes, even those imposing mandatory, non-probationable sentences, have not, for the most part, been enacted as to organized crime type offenses or offenders with the exception of drug trafficking offenses and habitual criminal sentencing statutes. Consequently, many believe that appropriate sentences have not been meted out to organized crime figures convicted of various offenses.

Efforts at elevating or increasing sentences for organized crime members frequently convicted of certain specified sentences have

---

[1]The President's Commission on Law Enforcement and Administration of Justice, *The Challenge of Crime in a Free Society: A Report*, p. 203 (Washington D.C., 1967).

[2]*Id.*

[3]Pennsylvania Crime Commission, *A Decade of Organized Crime: 1980 Report X* (St. Davids, Pennsylvania, 1980).

been made at both the federal and state levels. For example, Congress enacted as a portion of its Organized Crime Control Act of 1970[4] a special provision for the sentencing of certain "dangerous special offenders."[5] This provision, now codified in 18 U.S.C. § 3575, 3576, 3577, and 3578, generally provides a means to gain more stringent sentences for certain defendants including organized crime offenders. The sentencing court is impowered pursuant to the law to sentence a defendant for a term up to twenty-five years, "if it appears by a preponderance of the information, including information submitted during the trial of such felony and the sentencing hearing and . . . the presentence report . . . that the defendant is a dangerous special offender . . . "[6] The law, which does not prevent a sentence of death, life imprisonment, or incarceration in excess of twenty-five years if the underlying felony conviction so provides, is frequently used against organized crime defendants. Federal prosecutors who seek the use of this special sentencing statute may present wide information to the sentencing court "concerning the background, character, and conduct"[7] of the person to be sentenced pursuant to the law. If dissatisfied with the trial courts sentence imposition, prosecutors may, moreover, appeal that sentence to the United States Appeals Court for review.[8] Although the constitutionality of the statute has been challenged upon grounds that it can be invoked without indictment, that it is an ex post facto law, or bill of attainder, that it is violative of the double jeopardy clause, that it amounts to cruel and unusual punishment, or that it authorizes findings of fact based upon an impermissible standard of proof below proof beyond a reasonable doubt, the constitutionality of the law has been upheld by the courts (see, e.g., *United States v. Inendino*, 604 F. sd 458., 7th Cir., 444 U.S. 932, 1979; *United States v. Ilacqua*, 562 F. 2d 399, 6th Cir., *cert. denied,* 435 U.S. 906, 917, 947, 1977).

The necessary constitutional standard most frequently applied

---

[4]P.L. 91-452, 84 Statute 922 (October 15, 1970).

[5]15 U.S.C. §3575(b) (1970).

[6]15 U.S.C. §3575(b) (1970).

[7]15 U.S.C. § 3577 (1970).

[8]15 U.S.C. § 3576 (1970).

to such statutes was formulated early by the United States Supreme Court in *Weems v United States*, 217 U.S. 349 (1910). Such statues are often accused of violating the Eighth Amendment prohibition against cruel and unusual punishment that provides that "Excessive bail shall not be required, nor excessive fines imposed, nor cruel and unusual punishment inflicted." Quite generally, the Eighth Amendment standard as first interpreted by the *Weems* Court and refined in later years requires that legislated punishment fit the criminal act, compare favorably with punishments for similar offenses, and be supported by valid legislative purposes.[9]

Some state attempts at elevating punishment for certain offenses, including those for convicted organized crime members, have in some respects, been criticized.[10] Most often, state attempts to elevate punishment for certain offenders have concentrated upon repeat or habitual offenders. Such repeat or habitual offender statutes frequently provide for long-term (even life) sentences for conviction of as few as three offenses.[11] These statutes, which must pass the same constitutional requirements as the federal law above cited, are sometimes applied to organized crime members, so that repeat offenders are given longer prison terms upon a third, fourth, or greater number of convictions. The use of such legislation for confirmed organized crime members is clearly appropriate.

Aside from inadequacies in sentencing, meted out to organized crime members because of difficult sentencing statutes, problems sometimes abound because of the very nature of the defendants to be sentenced and because of the activities normally utilized by those defendants. The judiciary is not immune from the corrupt practices of organized crime defendants or the groups they represent. As the President's 1967 Crime Commission found: "There must be some kind of supervision over those trial judges who, because of corruption, political considerations, or lack of knowledge, tend to

---

[9]See, eg., *Hart v Coiner*, 483 F. 2d 136 (4th Circ., 1973).

[10]See "The Disparate Sentencing Provision of Ohio's Organized Crime Statutes," *46 CIN. L. REV.*, 583 (1976).

[11]See American Bar Association Report on Standards of Criminal Justice, *Standards Relating to Sentencing Alternatives and Procedures* (New York, Approved Draft, 1968).

mete out light sentences in cases involving organized crime management personnel."[12] Corruption, from its most obvious and gross
forms to its most subtle and almost imperceptible nuances, affects
judges just like it affects the rest of government. The effect at this
level, however, can frustrate and stymie the most effective investigation and prosecutorial efforts, even those that could properly be
characterized as ironclad. Consequently, efforts to monitor and
counter this form of corruption must be carried on continually.

Apart from questions surrounding the corruption of some members of the judiciary, other problems arise in the sentencing of
organized crime members. For example, such persons, even once
convicted, can quite readily provide very solid evidence of community ties, employment history, employability, property ownership,
marital and family stability, and similar evidence of societal
connections, all of which in the absence of mandatory sentencing
provisions greatly bolster, as we shall see, applications for probation and/or parole. The consequence of such ties, coupled with
corruption, the wide discretion afforded most judges, and the lack
of mandatory sentencing for organized crime cases, dictates moderate sentencing for the vast majority of organized crime members
who are convicted of one or more criminal acts. This of course
would not be true for more serious organized crime offenses such
as murder or kidnapping.

Normally, following any felony conviction a defendant so
convicted will make application for a presentence report and/or
application for probation. Almost invariably, such requests will be
granted, and the report so ordered will serve as the foundation for
any sentencing decision or subsequent probation order. Frequently,
organized crime members, particularly those associated with La
Cosa Nostra, can provide very solid evidence of probationability
and even if sentenced can provide evidence that they will be a
good parole risk. As a consequence, many of these individuals are
granted probation and/or parole even though they may have a
background literally steeped in organized crime participation.
Often, these members do not have lengthy criminal records but
only organized crime involvement, which for the most part is

---

[12]*Report, supra*, note 1.

difficult to document during the course of criminal proceedings as well as sentencing hearings.

Frequently, sentencing decisions associated with organized crime members do not live up to the expectations of law enforcement officers who originally investigated and/or analyzed the cases. Often, the claim is that the sentence is too light for the real essence of the offense. Such claims are sometimes valid but subject in some cases to misplaced criticism. The normal sentencing process, set in place for all sentencing decisions, relies upon a court bureaucracy to provide investigations and recommendations for all offenders including those associated with organized crime. The system frequently relies upon normal standards such as those enunciated heretofore to provide insight into sentencing recommendations and decisions. As a consequence, the power and wealth of most organized crime members benefit from these standards inasmuch as in most cases members of these groups can quite readily meet those standards.

Prosecutors are most often relied upon to provide recommendations for most sentencing decisions including those associated with organized crime cases. Such recommendations should focus on the organized crime member's past criminal activities, even though there may be a lack of formal arrest and/or conviction. The intelligence system discussed heretofore can greatly assist in sentencing decisions in providing information to prosecutors to in turn make recommendations to the court. Often, at sentencing hearings witnesses can be presented to testify as to a defendant's past activities and behavior. The rules are not quite as stringent in sentencing hearings as in criminal trials and, as a consequence, much valuable information can sometimes be presented to the court by an aggressive prosecutor armed with intelligence data indicating past criminal activity. Continuing efforts must be made by prosecutors and law enforcement officers to provide relevant data to judges making sentencing decisions.

Judges frequently have the power and authority to levy fines and in appropriate cases order the seizure of property owned by organized crime members upon application and proper pleading by the state. Given these circumstances, sentencing decisions should concentrate not only upon providing jail and prison time for organized crime members but also such decisions should focus upon financial punishment, thereby depriving the fruits of organized crime's labor to its members.

Some sentencing decisions exercised by members of the judiciary, however, ultimately contribute to the continuing growth of organized crime. For example, it has been found that certain ethnic organized crime groups solidify very strong ties among their group members while in prison. This is particularly true as to Hispanics, Blacks, and certain other minority gangs.[13] In such cases, prison sentences only serve to make certain organized crime groups stronger and to solidify the ties among the group's members. Whereas the Mafia has managed to solidify its relationship among group members through family and ethnic ties, the prison system has managed to solidify relationships among certain of these organized crime minority gangs. Efforts should be made in sentencing decisions, when appropriate, upon examination and investigation, to segregate members of such groups so that continuing ties and contacts can be kept to a minimum.

It has been suggested that prison sentences for certain actual or potential organized crime members, particularly for specific minority groups, serve to solidify associations among groups or network members: "[P]rison is ... important in network organization (organized crime groups affiliation) among Blacks and Puerto Ricans ... [T]he primary importance of prison in the formation of [such groups] ... has been confirmed by ... observations [of certain] networks. ... Friendships among [such] criminals ... formed [either early] in childhood gangs ... and validated in common prison experience [or through initial contact in prison] ... tend to be very personal and consequently tend to be lasting. They have the character of partnerships since they depend on mutual trust and responsibility as well as compatability of the individuals."[14] Prison sentences in such situations, even when viewed as necessary and unavoidable evils, serve to strengthen and perhaps harden certain organized crime associations.[15]

---

[13]F. Ianni, *Ethnic Succession in Organized Crime: Summary Report 6* (Washington D.C., 1973).

[14]*Id.*

[15]*Id.*

Even in circumstances where organized crime members have in fact been sentenced to penal institutions, evidence is sometimes uncovered indicating the presence of organized crime group hierarchy within penal systems. In fact, over the years, evidence has been provided indicating that certain members of organized crime groups have managed to continue overseeing their criminal operations from prison. A clear communication system, for example, has been in some cases discovered that allows the transmittal and receipt of messages regarding organized crime activities. Moreover, organized crime members, with their wealth, in-prison and out-of-prison connections, and reputations, are in positions to undermine the formal structure of any penal institution, creating inmate organized crime groups within the prison that monopolize illicit services and commodities demanded by the inmate population. The same activities that organized crime frequently carries on outside the penal system are therefore carried on inside the penal system, whereby certain desired but illicit commodities and/or services are provided for a given monetary or other payment.

Following sentencing decisions, or grants of probation and/or ultimate parole, continuing efforts should be made through the probation department, if possible, to monitor the activities of a discharged or probationed organized crime member. Often, during the course of probation or parole supervision, information regarding the activities and continuing operations of individuals can be obtained. With organized crime individuals, there is generally little hope of rehabilitation, and as a consequence law enforcement should make some effort to concentrate on acquiring information to assist in ongoing criminal investigations and to determine whether or not such members have violated their probation and/or parole. In such circumstances information not only should be obtained from the probation or parole department but also passed on to those departments where appropriate.

Sentencing decisions regarding organized crime members have generally resulted in somewhat more lenient punishment by the court system for organized crime activities. This has come about through a wide variety of individual factors and considerations as we have discussed. Efforts should be continually made, however, by prosecutorial personnel and law enforcement officers to keep the judiciary and the public informed of the true nature of organized crime activity and the true activities of its members. In this regard, a better informed public will make more sophisticated demands upon the judiciary for appropriate punishment in organized crime cases. Moreover, prosecutorial efforts should be undertaken at the sentencing hearing to provide relevant information when available as to an individual's ongoing, historical organized crime associations and memberships. In this way a true picture can be presented to the court along with recommendations designed not only to punish the particular member by incarcerating such a member for a period of time but also to fine that individual and/or seize property used by that individual in organized crime operations. Efforts must also be undertaken to guard against subtle corruption of members of the judiciary, and perhaps this too can be accomplished through an informed and involved public and law enforcement community.

Section V

Conclusions and Recommendations

Organized crime has often been referred to as a cancer or malignancy eating away at the very fiber of our society. The problem, as we have seen, is not limited to America but rather is international in scope. The malignancy or cancer that has been eating away at our society continues to do so each day. The activities of organized crime (even though often providing desired commodities or services) threaten our democratic government as well as the vitality of our economic system.

Organized crime has managed to exist over the years through murder, force, and intimidation, as well as bribery and corruption of public officials. Without the actual neutralization and negation of government and the subversion of the governmental process to serve its own ends, organized crime could not exist. Corruption is a key element when considering the continued existence of the phenomenon.

As we have seen, organized crime is more than the Mafia, more than La Cosa Nostra, and more than the emerging organized crime groups discussed in preceding chapters. Organized crime is really a loose-knit organization of deviant societal and criminal elements that feed upon human weakness and strive to achieve power and profit through manipulation of those weaknesses. Although we have seen the difficulty in attempting to systematically and accurately define the phenomenon, it is quite clear that the problem crosses not only ethnic lines but all similar clear-cut generalizations.

Of late, the study and public awareness of the problem of organized crime has been in the forefront, due in part to law enforcement efforts to eradicate the problem and prosecute its participants. Moreover, recent Valachi-style public and courtroom revelations by another, but higher-level member of La Cosa Nostra,

James Fratianno, together with deep penetrating law enforcement undercover operations, have brought many organized crime leaders to successful prosecution. Many of these individuals have been sentenced to prison or are awaiting such sentencing as of this writing. In light, however, of the hierarchical organizational structure of most organized crime groups, the elimination of leadership in such groups merely results in an increased upward mobility for lower echelon members of the group who rise up the "corporate" ladder when vacancies are thus created. Whether or not these recent, although successful, prosecutorial efforts ultimately and successfully affect organized crime groups as a social phenomenon remains to be seen. While the Reagan administration has committed itself to the obliteration of the problem of organized crime, such a result seems unlikely in light of the historical, sociological, and economic factors involved. Organized crime, as we have seen, has existed for hundreds of years largely due to its ability to capitalize upon human weakness and profit from those weaknesses while keeping government and the risk of punishment at bay through corruption of public officials. Moreover, when considering the wealth, power, and influence of all organized crime groups, it may be that the enforcement community is simply not capable of effectively obliterating the problem; however, continued enforcement efforts should be able to diminish the power, influence, and profits of organized crime.

Some have suggested that the real answer to the elimination of organized crime lies with the populace as a whole. In this country organized crime is regarded by many as a "service industry" supplying what is frequently desired and, as a consequence, often exposing the seamy and debased side of human personality and its weaknesses. Some citizens, for example, see nothing wrong with many of the activities of organized crime such as gambling, fencing, or prostitution. However, a combined and intensive educational and informational dissemination program would help, over time, to change or adjust public attitudes regarding organized crime and its activities. Any effective law enforcement or societal effort to deal with the problem must include this significant aspect. Answers, some contend, can only be found in the populaces' wallets and collective conscience.[1] The problem, still others believe, "will continue [until] ... a lot of honest Americans decide it's time to put a stop to it."[2]

In the end, one can only conclude, as many have done heretofore, that the mob is winning and will continue to win unless a thorough and comprehensive program to eliminate or diminish the extent of the problem is launched by all segments of the government and society. Such a program must include, at a minimum, the following:

1. Public educational and informational awareness of the true organized crime problem, including all of its activities, effects, and costs.
2. Law enforcement allocation of sufficient resources, including competently and thoroughly trained personnel to engage in systematic efforts to uncover and ultimately prosecute or otherwise adversely affect organized crime groups.
3. Governmental provision of resources, including not only funds but legislative enforcement tools to assist law enforcement in its efforts to deal with the problem of organized crime.
4. Business cooperation with government and law enforcement in joint efforts to stop or curtail the infiltration of legitimate business and the undermining of the entire economic system.
5. Public recruitment of more dedicated, sincere, and honest public officials, who will be more resistant to corruption.

Although these conclusions may seem to be readily apparent, the task of achieving these goals will not be made any simpler by reason of any apparent ease in conclusion, recognition, or identification. One can only hope that the efforts now underway, including the systematic approach to training taken in this text, will help to meet the problems head-on and ultimately diminish and overcome a most sinister and seamy side of our society.

---

[1]"Crashing on Cocaine", *Time Magazine* (April 11, 1983, p. 31).

[2]Editorial, *The Repository*, (Monday, January 3, 1983, p. 4).

BIBLIOGRAPHY

Books

American Bar Association Project on Standards for Criminal Justice, *Standards Relating to Electronic Surveilance* (American Bar Association, 1968).

American Bar Association Project on Standards for Criminal Justice, *Standards Relating to the Function of Trial Judge* (American Bar Association, 1972 Approved Draft).

American Bar Association Project on Standards for Criminal Justice, *Standards Relating to Sentencing Alternatives and Procedures* (American Bar Association, 1968 Approved Draft).

American Bar Association Project on Standards for Criminal Justice, *Standards Relating to Probation* (American Bar Association, 1970, Approved Draft).

F. Carrington and W. Lambie, *The Defenseless Society* (Greenville Publishers, Inc., Ottawa, Illinois, 1976).

Chamber of Commerce of the United States, *Textbook on Organized Crime* (Chamber of Commerce of the United States, 1972).

R. Clark, *Crime in America* (Simon and Schuster, New York, 1970).

J. Conklin, ed., *The Crime Establishment* (Prentice Hall, Inc., Englewood Cliffs, New Jersey, 1973).

D. Cressey, *Criminal Organization: Its Elementary Forms* (Harper and Row Publishers, New York, 1972).

D. Cressey, *Theft of the Nation: The Structure and Operations of Organized Crime in America* (Harper and Row Publishers, New York, 1969).

A. Darual, *A History of Secret Societies* (Cidatel Press, New York, 1961).

O. Demaris, *The Last Mafiosa* (Bantam Books, New York, 1981).

E. Godfrey, Jr., and D. Harris, *Basic Elements of Intelligence: A Manual of Theory, Structure and Procedures for Use by Law Enforcement Agencies Against Organized Crime* (U.S. Government, Washington D.C., 1971).

R. Hammer, *Playboy's Illustrated History of Organized Crime* (Playboy Press, Chicago, Illinois, 1975).

D. Harris, *Basic Elements of Intelligence, Revised Edition* (L.E.A.A., Washington D.C., 1976 Revised Edition).

C. Hicks, *Uniform Regulations Governing Informants* (Orange County, California, 1973).

F. Homer, *Guns and Garlic* (Purdue University Press, West Lafayette, Indiana, 1974).

229

IIT Research Institute and the Chicago Crime Commission, *A Study of Organized Crime in Illinois* (Chicago, Illinois, 1971).

F. Ianni, *Ethnic Succession in Organized Crime, Summer Report* (L.E.A.A., Washington D.C., 1973).

F. Ianni, *The Black Mafia* (Simon and Schuster, New York, 1974).

Illinois Legislative Investigating Commission, *The Illicit Traffic in Stolen Securities, A Report to the Illinois General Assembly* (Chicago, Illinois, October, 1973).

C. Klockars, *The Professional Fence* (The Free Press, New York, 1974).

H. Lamb, *The Crusades* (The Literary Guild of America, Inc., New York, 1940).

The Law Enforcement Consulting Committee—1982, *Report to the Governor of Ohio on Organized Crime* (Columbus, Ohio, 1982).

L.E.A.A., *Police Guide on Organized Crime* (L.E.A.A., Washington D.C., 1972).

P. Maas, *The Valachi Papers* (G. P. Putnam & Sons, New York, 1968).

A. McCoy et al., *The Politics of Heroin in Southeast Asia* (Harper and Row Publishers, New York, 1972).

National Advisory Committee on Criminal Justice Standards and Goals, *Organized Crime: Report to the Task Force on Organized Crime* (Washington D.C., 1976).

The National Association of Attorney's General, Committee on the Office of Attorney General, *Organized Crime Control Legislation* (January, 1975).

National Association of Attorney's General, Committee on the Office of Attorney General, *Organized Crime Controlled Seminar Book* (Albuquerque, New Mexico, April 28, April 29, 1975).

The National Association of Attorney's General, Committee on the Office of Attorney General, *Organized Crime Controlled Units* (June, 1975).

National Association of Attorney's General, Committee on the Office of Attorney General, *Organized Crime Controlled Special Report: The Use of Civil Remedies in Organized Crime Control* (Raleigh, North Carolina, December, 1975).

National College of District Attorneys, *Proceedings: Advanced Organized Crime Seminar* (Houston, Texas December, 1974).

The National Institute of Law Enforcement and Criminal Justice, *The Nature, Impact and Prosecution of White Collar Crime* (U.S. Department of Justice, L.E.A.A., Washington D.C., 1970).

State of Ohio, Organized Crime Prevention Council, *Systems One Seminar—1975* (Columbus, Ohio, 1975).

Ohio Law Enforcement Consulting Committee, *A Report and Recommendations for Dealing with Organized Crime in Ohio and Indiana* (Columbus, Ohio, October, 1975).

Ohio Law Enforcement Consulting Committee, *Ohio Organized Crime Counsel Law Enforcement Consulting Committee Progress Report* (Columbus, Ohio, October, 1976).

Ohio Organized Crime Prevention Council, *System Two 1975 Seminar* (Columbus, Ohio, 1975).

Ohio Organized Crime Prevention Council, *System Two 1976 Seminar* (Columbus, Ohio, 1976).

H. Overstreet and B. Overstreet, *The FBI in Our Open Society* (W. W. Norton and Company, New York, 1969).

Pennsylvania Crime Commission, *A Decade of Organized Crime: 1980 Report* (St. Davids, Pennsylvania, 1980).

T. Plate, *The Mafia at War* (The New York Magazine Press, New York, 1972).

The President's Commission on Law Enforcement and Administration of Justice, Task Force on Organized Crime, *Task Force Report: Organized Crime* (Washington D.C., 1967).

The President's Commission on Law Enforcement and Administration of Justice, *The Challenge of Crime in a Free Society: A Report* (Washington D.C., 1967).

R. Salerno and J. Tompkins, *The Crime Confederation* (Doubleday Company and Inc., Garden City, New York, 1969).

E. Schur, *Our Criminal Society* (Prentice Hall, Inc., Englewood Press, New Jersey, 1969).

D. Smith, *The Mafia Mystique* (Basic Books, Inc., New York, 1975).

W. Whalen, *Handbook of Secret Organizations* (The Bruce Publishing Company, Milwaukee, Wisconsin, 1966).

Periodicals

Beck, et al., *"The Toxic Waste Crisis,"* Newsweek (p. 20, March 7, 1983).

Comment, "The Disparate Sentencing Provision of Ohio's Organized Crime Statute," 46 *CINCINNATI LAW REVIEW*, 83 (n.d.).

Cook, "Organized Crime: Unregulated, Untaxed, Unstopable, The Invisible Enterprise," *Forbes Magazine* 60 (September 29, 1980).

Cook, "The Invisible Enterprise, Part II: Money Makes the Mob Go Round," *Forbes Magazine* 120 (October 13, 1980).

Cook, "The Invisible Enterprise — Part III: Casino Gambling: Changing Character or Changing Fronts," *Forbes Magazine* 89 (October 27, 1980)

Cook, "The Invisible Enterprise — Part IV: The Most Abused, Misabused Pension Fund in America," *Forbes Magazine* 126 (November 10, 1980).

Dowd, Jr., "The Warrant Handbook For Prosecutors and Law Enforcement Officers," (Canton, Ohio, October, 1974).

Goettel, "Why the Crime Syndicate Can't Be Touched," 221 *Harper's Magazine* 34 (November, 1960).

Harper and Harris, "The Application of Link Analysis to Police Intelligence," 17 *Human Factors* 157 (1975).

Herbert, "The Criminal Justice and Information Act: A Proposal Which Will Affectively Terminate Investigations of Organized Crime," 12 *Police Times* 9 (June, 1977).

Herbert, "The Use of Link Network Analysis As A Trial Technique In the Prosecution of Organized Crime Cases," (Appendix 2) *Systems Two — 1976* (Ohio Organized Crime Prevention Council Seminar, Columbus, Ohio, 1976).

Herbert, "The Use of Minors as Undercover Agents or Informants: Some Legal

Problems," 5 *J. Pol. Sci. & Admin.*, 185 (June 1977).

Kefauver, "Crime in America," 17 *VITAL SPEECHES* 655 (August 15, 1951).

Kelly, "War Against Organized Crime is Being Won," *U.S. News and World Report* 50 (April 8, 1974).

Lippmann, "The Underworld: A Stultified Conscience, 85 *Forum* 65 (February, 1931).

Lippmann, "The Underworld: Our Secret Servant," 85 *Forum* 1 (January, 1931).

McClellan, "Organized Crime in the United States," 35 *Vital Speeches* 388 (April 15, 1969).

Press, "The New Mafia," *Newsweek* 34 (January 5, 1981).

Salerno, "Banking and Organized Crime," 154 *The Bankers Magazine*, 59 Spring (1971).

Salerno, "New Crime Threat: The Black Mafia," *Ohio Organized Crime's Systems One 1975 Seminar* (Ohio Organized Crime Prevention Council, Columbus, Ohio, 1975).

Salerno, "Organized Crime, an Unmet Challenge to Criminal Justice," *Crime and Delinquency* (1969).

Salerno, "The Classic Pattern of Organized Crime," *Systems One—1975 Seminar* (Ohio Organized Crime Prevention Council, Columbus, Ohio, 1975).

Schelling, "What is the Business of Organized Crime?" 110 *The American Scholar* 643, Autumn, 1979.

Smith, Jr., and Salerno, "The Use of Strategies in Organized Crime Control," 61 *The Journal of Criminal Law, Criminology and Police Science* 101 (1970).

"War On Organized Crime Takes a New Turn: Organized Crime and Racketeering Strike Forces," *U.S. News and World Report* 64 (May 31, 1976).

INDEX

Italic page numbers indicate pages on which figures appear.